Don't Give Up On Me...
I'm Not Finished Yet!

Don't Give Up On Me...
I'm Not Finished Yet!

*Putting the Finishing Touches
On the Person You Want to Be*

Ray S. Anderson

McCracken Press
New York

McCracken Press™
An imprint of Multi Media Communicators, Inc.
575 Madison Avenue, Suite 1006
New York, NY 10022

McCracken Press™ is a trademark of Multi Media Communicators, Inc.

Cover by Jim Hellman

Library of Congress Cataloging-in-Publication Data

Anderson, Ray Sherman.
    Don't give up on me...I'm not finished yet!; putting
the finishing touches on the person you want to be /
Ray S. Anderson. — 1st ed.
        p .   cm.
    Includes bibliographical references.
    ISBN 1-56977-607-5: $14.95
    1. Self-help techniques. 2. Self-actualization (Psychology)
I. Title.
BF632.A65 1993   94-7485
158' . 1—dc20   CIP

10 9 8 7 6 5 4 3 2 1

Printed in the United States of America

Contents

PART THREE

Self-Recovery: The Journey To Freedom

Introduction

"Wait a minute, I'm not finished yet," was the impatient response from my five-year-old daughter when I once tried to get her to leave her coloring book and come to dinner. She is now a grown woman with two children of her own. "I'm not finished yet. . . ." I hope she still feels that way!

The struggle for recovery is not to overcome the hindrances and problems that beset us yesterday and today, but to become the person that we can be tomorrow. In other words, "Wait a minute, I'm not finished yet!"

The goal of recovery is not to emerge from an abusive relationship or traumatic experience as a battle-scarred survivor but as a passionate lover of life. In other words, "Wait a minute, I'm not finished yet!"

The gift of recovery is more than being plucked out of a whirlpool of emotional distress and planted in a quiet lagoon where the water is so shallow that no wave breaks the surface. Recovery means more than being cast as a survivor upon some deserted beach with the hope that the small island of safety will provide all that is necessary to be self-sufficient. The gift of recovery is to have the sails repaired, the rudder restored, and one's hand on the tiller with a spanking breeze and a spacious horizon. In other words, "Wait a minute, I'm not finished yet!"

Beginning the Journey

What more and more people have in common today is recovery. If you are struggling to overcome a self defeating pattern of life, or you are crying out for healing from a grievous loss, you are in recovery. When you discover that you are not the only one who has suffered from abuse, a failed marriage, chemical dependency, or tragic loss and grief, you are ready to begin the journey toward recovery.

Contemporary recovery movements tend to focus on recovery *from* dysfunctional and crippling experiences in the past. This is a much needed emphasis. There must be healing before there can be hope. In becoming the person we were meant to be we must overcome the cruel and crippling blows which we have suffered in the past. The past cannot be changed, but we can grow out of it toward a future that brings self-fulfillment. Recovery begins when we stop making promises to ourselves and reach out toward the promise of life intended for us by our Creator.

True self-recovery moves beyond overcoming a problem to becoming a whole person. The human self is oriented toward a destiny which influences and shapes the present as much or more than the origins and early experiences of the self. This orientation leads to an emphasis on recovery *toward* the wholeness, health and happiness that God intends for each person.

Recovery is a process that begins with *overcoming* and leads to *becoming*. Recovery is a movement of the self from where we have *been* to where we want to *be*. It is a journey toward the recovery of a self that was pledged to us in the blessing of birth and promised to us as a goal to be gained.

We are all beginners on the journey to self-recovery!

Begin with the Self

This is not just another self-help book, though it is a beginner's guide to self-recovery. We must have some knowledge of ourselves, our feelings, our emotions, our divinely endowed potential, before we can begin the process of self-care. We must discover the secret of empowerment before we attempt to escape the seduction of entrapment. We must experience the worth of our own life before we can value the life of others. We must learn how to grieve our losses before we can discover the growing edge of a better life.

In reading this book you will learn how to begin the process of self-recovery. You will experience recovery of self-worth, emotional health, and a strong and vital faith in the face of life's inevitable and sometimes irrational pain and suffering.

My approach is grounded in the Judeo-Christian tradition of humans created in the image and likeness of God. The critical need for persons in recovery is an understanding of the nature and capacity of the human self for self-recovery, given the resources of divine grace and the competent assistance and support of others.

I write as a theologian—one who looks for authentic humanity through the lens of divine revelation. I also write as a pastoral counselor—one who seeks the wisdom of God through the tangled web of human experience.

For those with religious convictions, the experience of suffering, the pervading presence of evil, and devastating and tragic losses in life can produce a crisis of faith. Ultimately, the questions which arise out of injury to the self through failure, loss, and abuse become religious questions. In the struggle to find meaning and purpose in life, God is the one we hold to be finally accountable. This is because the depth of human pain points to the height of human aspiration.

Self-recovery touches the depth of our despair in order to reach the height of our happiness. The self in recovery stretches the boundaries of faith and strengthens the heart to believe. As the English playwright Christopher Fry once wrote,

> The human heart can go to the lengths of God. . . .
> Affairs are now soul size.
> The enterprise
> Is exploration into God.[1]

"Wait a minute," my daughter said, "I'm not finished yet!" And wait we did. She was just beginning the journey, and we were not far down the road ourselves. Reading this book will not make you an expert, but it will be a guide to your beginning. Join me as we go together.

PART ONE

SELF-UNDERSTANDING:

The Secret of Empowerment

CHAPTER ONE

Trust Your Feelings

"I am an emotional wreck." So began the conversation with a student who had made an appointment with me to discuss an academic matter. "What does that feel like?" I responded. She paused a long time, and then said, "I feel like an abandoned child." "What caused this feeling," I inquired. She went on to recount several instances of rejection by her parents and physical abuse by her former husband.

As we talked she was amazed to discover that her emotional tailspin was not a freefall into an abyss, but that beneath the emotions of anger, self-loathing, and fear that she was out of control, was a quite specific feeling which had a basis in fact. "Feelings don't lie," I told her. "They will tell you the truth, painful as it is."

Feelings Do Not Lie

Strange, that we should trust the mind which so often deceives us and distrust the feelings which lead directly to the core of the self. "Lean on the facts, not your feelings," we are warned when attempting to resolve some inner doubt and uncertainty over a decision.

"My eyes played tricks on me," we say when forced to admit that what we thought we saw was actually a misperception. It was our mind, not our eyes, that misled us. When we think something we tend to see it that way. It is not our feelings that misled us, it is the idea or concept that we attribute to those feelings.

Feelings are an essential and accurate expression of the self, says Dr. Archibald Hart, Professor of Psychology at the Fuller Seminary Graduate School of Psychology. While our emotions may be distorted by making incorrect interpretations of what we experience, feelings are connected directly to the self and serve as a guide to restoring the unity and health of the self.[1]

Can I trust my feelings? Yes, though you cannot stay with your feelings. You can trust your feelings to bring you "to your senses." When feelings are painful there has been or continues to be a stimulation to the senses that produced the feeling. Feelings do not lie. Feelings tell us when we have been hurt, or when we have suffered a loss to the self. Feelings direct us to the issue that caused the feeling. Harmful and abusive stimulations of the self need to be identified and removed where possible. Where it is not possible, rouse the resources of the entire self with all of its repertoire of feelings and mount a defense.

Where the stimulation which produced the feeling has long been removed, feelings need to be healed. Feelings cannot be changed by thinking differently about them, they need to be healed. The source of healing a hurt feeling is the inner life of the self from which a new feeling can emerge. The recovery of the self begins with unleashing the power of feelings to produce a new and positive one.

Feelings are the Self

Feelings may be the most critical indicators of well-being that we possess. The feelings that we acquire as infants and children form the matrix of the self for our adult years. Feelings need care and nurturing as much, if not more, than the physical parts of the self. When our feelings are sick, there is no good health. When feelings are wounded we suffer pain. When feelings diminish, we lose contact with the world and our relationships with others. Depression becomes a warning signal that our feelings are being repressed and our self is closing down.

Feelings are produced through sensations which stimulate a variety of feelings. The five senses—touch, sight, sound, taste, smell—orient the self to its environment. Perhaps there is also a "sixth sense," a stimulation of the self not easily recognized or identified by the other senses. The uncanny feeling that some presence is near us can cause, as it were, "the hair to rise on the back of our neck!"

These sensations are registered by the self as feelings prior to any self-conscious awareness or thought. The unborn child in the womb demonstrates reflexes to stimuli and thus may also experience feelings. With the removal of the sensation, the feeling remains as part of the undifferentiated prenatal self. These feelings form the core of the self as a living, sentient, and responding organism.

When I say, "I feel sad," it is fully equivalent to, "I *am* sad." When we arouse feelings in someone, we arouse the real self. When we track an emotion to its source we discover a feeling. Because feelings are triggered by sensations, they are never wrong, though not always pleasant.

Feelings, therefore, are more than sensations produced by external stimuli. Feelings are more than emotions which flood the terrain of the inner self. Feelings *are* the self as a living and experiencing being. Where the self exists feelings are present, even if unrecognized or unexpressed. Where feelings are present, the self exists *as* the feelings, not alongside or apart from the feelings.

The earliest responses of infants to the attention of others do not always require touch. Using all of its senses, the infant experiences itself through the stimulation of smells, sounds, and visual images as well as touch. The core of the self in the infant actively responds to the self of the other through feelings. Infants can actually *feel* the presence of another without being touched. These feelings are not merely sensations which the self has, as though there is an unfeeling self hidden behind the responsive self. The feelings *are* the self, and the capacity to respond to the presence of another is the capacity to feel. This response means growth for the self when the presence represents love and care.

When feelings as the response capacity of the self are nurtured and encouraged, touch can also produce the feeling of happiness and pleasure. It is the intrinsic longing of the self for fulfillment which underlies the pleasure seeking instinct. By reinforcing this sense of pleasure, infants begin to develop a sense of the self and a capacity to interpret the sensory experiences of life as either pleasant or unpleasant, a life-long process.

Feelings are Self-Perceptions

In the diary of a girl not yet twelve, named Opal by her foster parents, the precocious thoughts of a child who experienced her self as "feeling" surprise us with their clarity and truth:

Now are come the days of leaves.
They talk with the wind.
I hear them tell of their borning days.
They whisper of the hoods they wear.
Today they talk of the time
before their borning days.
They tell how they were part of the earth
and the air before their tree-borning days.
In grey days of winter
they go back to earth again.
But they do not die.
I saw a silken cradle in a hazel branch.
It was cream with a hazel leaf
halfway around it.
I put it to my ear and I did listen.
It had a little voice.
It was a heart voice.
While I did listen, I did feel its feels.
It has lovely ones.
I did hurry to the house of the girl
who has no seeing
so she might know its feels
and hear its heart voice.
She does so like to feel things.
She has seeing by feels.[2]

Feelings are like an iceberg, nine-tenths of them may lie below the surface of consciousness. We may think that we have no feelings, or that we have our feelings under control, but then find ourselves acting and reacting in ways that betray the power of these submerged feelings. The small child, Opal, having lost both parents at the age of five and placed in a foster home of a family working the Oregon lumber camps at the turn of the century, cultivated her experience of self with respect to her world of animals, trees, and flowers at a depth of feeling which threatened to burst through her limited vocabulary like an erupting gusher. "While I did listen," she tells us, "I did feel its feels."

Where do feelings go when they sink into the self and are lost to conscious memory? Are they like names and numbers which we memorize to retain in the mind for future reference, but which often disappear without a trace?

Are feelings stuck to the self like the Post-Its we use to call our attention to important tasks—notes that can be easily removed without leaving a blemish?

Are feelings like coastal clouds that creep in overnight only to be driven back over the ocean by the heat of the morning sun? Sometimes it seems that the same feelings drift into our soul over and over again as though borne by invisible currents over which we have no control. In this case, the feelings may disappear for a time, but never vanish.

What psychologists call the "unconscious" may be feelings which cannot be directly identified or processed by the self at the conscious level of thought. These "unconscious" feelings often come to expression in our behavior without any "logical" explanation. Or, they may appear in symbolic form in our dreams. We can experience these deep feelings even though we may never be able to think about them or communicate them to others.

For example, many of us have had experiences which have a certain mystical quality about them. I have had a sense of being "moonstruck" when the immensity and power of a moonbeam slicing through the night seemed to be aimed right at the core of my being, connecting me with some invisible and intangible reality I could not explain.

People have been known to weep at the playing of a childhood tune long forgotten. Lovers tremble and friends fall silent in the sudden and incredible shock of the presence of the *other* as though a curtain has been lifted momentarily and the undiluted spirit of another soul breathes upon us. One of the early astronauts, when orbiting the earth, looked out at the slowly spinning globe in space which he called home and had an experience so deeply personal and spiritual that it transformed his life forever.

How Feelings Form the Self

His name is Brogan. He is twenty months old and he is my youngest grandson. He was quietly suspicious of me when he was carried off the airplane by his father for a short visit only 24 hours earlier. Already he trusts me to hold him. I raise him high above my head and he giggles with pleasure at the sudden acceleration of his body. We roll on the carpet and he climbs on my back to "ride horse." When I collapse in feigned exhaustion, he cries out, "more!"

We play in the park, feed the ducks, and pretend that he is running away and I can barely run fast enough to catch him. He calls me Papa, and for just a brief moment looks into my eyes with pure love and trust. It is, for me at least, and I think for him, an experience that psychologists call bonding. Like two gulls swooping across a sunlit meadow, our winged souls touch in flight. We both sense the presence of the other and feel the sudden stab of recognition that yields a pleasure almost too painful to bear.

Then it strikes me. He will not remember this moment nor hold for long the image of my face in his mind. For a few weeks perhaps, aided by a picture and some parental prompting, he will give the correct answer when quizzed about a name and face. But a few months later, his growing mind will be filled with names and events more familiar to hand and eye. It struck me with a sadness that I could scarcely comprehend. He will not remember this moment nor remember me when his childhood feelings give way to a more permanent self-consciousness.

When we meet again I will enter his familiar world as a stranger and we will need to become friends once again. Yes I know, the bonding may well be there, so the psychologists tell me. But I want Brogan to tell me! I want him to remember, not just my face, but his own feelings of shared joy and love. When he is older, I will tell him the story, of course, and he will believe it. But he will likely never recover the feelings that became so much a part of the self that he now recognizes as his own.

When he awakens to himself, like all of us, he will ponder the mystery of those years between his birth and his awakening. Part of the self remains silent and never speaks, no matter how fluent the vocabulary of the mind.

I read Annie Dillard. A Pulitzer Prize author who sees beneath the surface of life, Dillard exposes with surgical precision and exquisite grace the almost invisible connective tissue of feelings which link the self with its larger self-world. She goes as far as the self-conscious mind can go and peers with wonder at the mystery of the self awakening to self-consciousness.

> Children ten years old wake up and find themselves here, discover themselves to have been here all along; is this sad? They wake like sleepwalkers, in full stride; they wake like people brought back from cardiac arrest or from drowning: *in medias res*, surrounded by familiar people and objects, equipped with a hundred skills. They know the neighborhood, they can read and write English, they are old hands at the commonplace mysteries, and yet they feel themselves to have just stepped off the boat, just converged with their bodies, just flown down from a trance, to lodge in an eerily familiar life already well under way.

I woke in bits, like all children, piecemeal over the years. I discovered myself and the world, and forgot them, and discovered them again. I woke at intervals until, by that September when Father went down the river, the intervals of waking tipped the scales, and I was more often awake then not. I noticed this process of waking, and predicted with terrifying logic that one of these years not far away I would be awake continuously and never slip back, and never be free of myself again.[3]

The overabundance of feelings that a not quite two-year-old experiences every hour of every day, many pleasurable and some painful, would last the ordinary person a lifetime! What happens to all of these feelings? Are they leached out of the self in the same way that fatigue disappears from weary muscles while we sleep? Or do they arise again and again to overwhelm us in the adult phase of our life?

Like Brogan, I had others to tell me the stories and fill in the gaps of my own pre-awakening years. But they could not make those silent feelings speak. Now all of those who attended me during those early years are gone. While they lived, they at least were witnesses to the fact that I did exist prior to the knowledge of my existence. I had depended on others to sustain the continuity of my awakening self to my birth self. I could build my life around the conscious self, but not around the feelings which receded into the subconscious realm. Having discovered memory as a construct of the mind, I took no thought of feelings which could not be remembered. Because the years lost to my memory could not be recalled, I assumed that the feelings were lost as well.

A man recently explained to me why he ended a marriage and walked away from the relationship by saying, "I lost all feeling for her." In this case, the loss of feelings was offered as a logical defense against the charge of abandoning a commitment. The positive feelings which he once admitted having were now gone. There was no expectation that these feelings could be recovered. He had many negative feelings toward her, as it turned out. Somehow these had acquired a value which he was not prepared to surrender. He had not lost all feelings toward her—only the ones which once drew him toward her.

When I experience my grandson in his frenzy of feelings I really come to *know* him, even though he does not yet know himself. Where do these feelings go when they disappear before the self can name them and claim them? They remain as part of an undifferentiated core of the self. When the stimulation is removed, the sensation ceases but the feeling remains.

For example, when Brogan held out a piece of bread to the duck in the park, the beak of the duck touched his finger in snatching the bread. Instantly he recoiled and cried out, "Duck bite me!" I took his finger and kissed it, though there was obviously no injury. The sensation of the duck's beak against his skin produced a strong feeling of fear more than one of pain. As we continued to play in the park, he would come up, hold out his finger, and say, "Duck bite me!" I would perform the ritual of kissing his finger, a stimulation which evidently produced a positive feeling which he now craved.

Where did the feeling of fear go when the stimulation caused by the duck's beak was replaced by the sensation of having his finger kissed? First of all, the fear was related to the duck's beak and not his finger. The feeling was his own immediate response to the sensation and when that feeling became attached to a new stimulation, comfort and assurance was felt.

Fear is like fatigue. When the muscle is able to relax,

the fatigue disappears. The self is like a muscle. It contracts and reacts to stimulation through feeling. The feeling does not go anywhere when the fear disappears. Rather, the feeling releases its grip on the fear and "lets go." This is why feeling itself is capable of restoration and recovery when negative and painful sensations are replaced by positive and supportive ones.

Precisely how we process the painful feelings which have become lodged in the self will become clear as we move into the second part of this book. What is important at this stage is the understanding of how feelings contribute to our emotions.

The Emotional Content of Feeling

We are now ready to clarify the subtle but important distinction between sensation, feeling, and emotion. *Sensations* are largely physiological responses to external stimuli. My muscles may tighten or my "skin crawl at some horrible stimuli." When I become aware of a sensation it is experienced as a *feeling*. The subjective element is now involved. This may be at a very low level of consciousness; I just *feel* something and am aware of the feeling. The emergence of self-consciousness with regard to a feeling does involve some level of thought to the degree that it registers with the self as "my feeling." I may then feel irritated, apprehensive, or become more attentive to the thing which caused the sensation.

From this it is clear that we can only articulate a feeling by expressing it as a thought. When we are unable to translate a feeling into a thought, we are unable to communicate it. We are then dependent upon someone else to intuit what the feeling is, but even then, if it is to be verified, it must be recognized as having the form of a concept.

We ask for reasons for emotions but not for feelings, because emotions can be shared as thoughts. Feelings are more difficult to share because they have to do more with sensation than with thought.

Suppose someone swings around with a piece of lumber in his hand and strikes me on the back of the head. If I do not see the action, my first response is a sensation of extreme pain. Subjectively, I immediately acknowledge this as a feeling of extreme distress, even though the sensation is almost entirely physiological. As I turn around to discover another person in the room with the board in his hand, I will experience anger. Anger is a strong emotion which is directed toward an object. If I assume that this injury was inflicted upon me intentionally, my anger becomes outrage and I add moral indignation to the feeling of pain. As an emotion, anger carries an attribution made by the thought process. The attribution is a judgment made that the injury was inflicted upon me by this person and my anger is directed toward him, not toward the point of the pain.

At this point, the person who struck me offers deep apologies and convinces me that it was an accident. He did not know that I was standing just behind him. On being persuaded that the blow was not intentional on his part, and with the moral judgment resolved by his taking responsibility for it and offering to do what is necessary to restore me to health, I alter the original attribution which led to the emotion of anger, and the anger dissipates.

I am still left with the feeling of pain, however, and will make some new attribution with regard to the feeling of pain resulting in a different emotion. Now, my emotion may be one of self-pity due to the fact that I have no one to blame but myself for not being more aware of my surroundings! Or, I may adopt a stoical attitude and attribute the accident to one of those things which cannot be prevented. "Accidents happen," I assure the person who struck me, "and I will be okay when the swelling goes down."

In this way, we see that emotions may be caused by an attribution which has no basis in fact. I felt anger as long as I assumed that I was intentionally hit. The emotion of anger can be changed with a new attribution which corresponds more nearly to the reality of the situation. Feelings, however, are deeper levels of the self than emotion and cannot be changed in the same way that we can change an emotion.

This is why feelings are a more accurate indication of the state of the self than emotions. At the same time, feelings cannot usually be distinguished from emotions because it is difficult to have a feeling without thinking about it! For this reason people tend to speak of feeling and emotion as being the same thing.

When the student collapsed into the chair and exclaimed, "I am an emotional wreck," she was honestly describing what most of us have felt like at times. She had the feeling that her emotional life was out of control. The beginning of her self-recovery was the discovery that her deepest feelings were based on real sensations and that her emotions were not as reliable as these feelings. Yet it was her emotions that were wrecking her life. The good news is that these emotions can be changed.

CHAPTER TWO

Regain Your
Emotional Strength

"I guess my problem is emotional," admitted a man who had come to me for pastoral counseling. "I'm having real problems at work and I think that my marriage is falling apart. I just can't seem to get a grip on my feelings. Sometimes I feel that if I started crying I would never stop. Then I get angry and lash out at the people that I can't afford to hurt."

He paused for a moment. I could see the contractions in his throat as he clenched his teeth and swallowed hard.

"The doctor tells me that I am under too much stress. But the thing that causes me the most stress is the feeling that I am losing control of my life. I remember that my mother once had what my father called a nervous breakdown and had to go into the hospital. I don't want that to happen to me."

Life is not kind to the emotionally handicapped. There are no privileged parking spaces at the supermarket. Inability to report to work due to emotional distress is not viewed with much understanding, and usually results in a wildfire of office gossip.

Emotional wounds do not bleed real blood, and dysfunction due to emotional upheaval does not merit a leave for recovery. For all of the fear of being told that one has a physical problem requiring surgery, it is of little comfort to have the doctor say, "Physically, there appears to be nothing wrong. The problem must be emotional."

When our emotions get out of control we are held hostage by our feelings. We start by blaming ourselves and end blaming others. Then, we assume the role of victim. Don't blame me for something over which I have no control!

The commonly accepted myth that emotions are like hormones, raging through our inner lives, out of control, is a cruel hoax perpetuated by conventional wisdom handed down from one generation to another.

It is time to unmask these myths and point the way toward recovery of misused emotions.

Emotional Myths and Misunderstandings

Myth #1: Emotions are bad.

The attachment of moral values to emotions probably stems from the involvement of emotion in our earliest behavior. When children are punished for actions which are judged unacceptable to adults, the emotions which led to the behavior and which occur as a result of the punishment are seldom acknowledged.

Few parents use sufficient discretion on this point. It requires considerable restraint to say to a child who has struck a sibling in a fit of anger, "That was very wrong to hurt your sister. I know that you were angry with her and you probably have reason to be. Let's find a way help her feel better." More typically, the response will be, "Johnny, that was a terrible thing to do and I'm going to take away your toy until you learn to control yourself."

The punishment is felt more keenly as disapproval of the emotion which led to the incident than for the act itself. The problem is compounded when the child is reprimanded by his father, "Son, stop crying about this. You know that what you did was wrong."

What we learn through repetition of experiences like this is that there are bad emotions as well as bad behavior. Anger, fear, self-pity, jealousy, and envy—these are just some of the emotions that are often considered to be bad, even sinful in some religious traditions.

The fact is, emotions have no moral value, either good or bad. Emotions may become unhealthy and impair our relationships with others as well as become destructive to our own sense of well-being, but they are neither good nor bad in a moral sense.

We should be held morally accountable for our intentions and actions, but not for our emotions. When we believe the myth that certain emotions are bad, then we will feel guilty for having the emotion rather than taking responsibility for our intentions and actions. Emotional guilt is the result of this emotional myth—I am a bad person because I have bad feelings. Freedom from this guilt begins with shattering the myth.

Myth #2: Showing emotion is a sign of weakness.

When a presidential candidate was shown weeping on television during a campaign a number of years ago, he was discredited in the eyes of many for this display of emotion. The incident was noted recently by a commentator as a sign that the general public becomes uneasy when a leader becomes overly emotional.

The cultural myth that strong persons do not demonstrate their feelings is probably based on a misunderstanding of emotion. If emotion is considered to be a sign that one can easily "lose control," then repression of one's feelings will be accepted as a mark of maturity and strength of character.

It has often been noted that most of the leading characters in the Bible, including Jesus himself, were persons who demonstrated strong feelings and even some emotional outbursts! Jeremiah is called the "weeping prophet." David, in many of his Psalms, expresses a depth of grief, anger, sorrow, and outrage that goes beyond what we find acceptable in our own lives, not to mention our leaders!

The emotions of God include jealousy, anger, tenderness, outrage, and unrestrained joy. One of the most poignant and powerful texts in the New Testament is the description of Jesus at the tomb of Lazarus: "Jesus began to weep" (John 11:35).

Contrary to the myth that emotion is a sign of weakness, the feelings which underlie our emotions provide flexibility in responding to the wide range of experiences which confront the self. Extreme rigidity and inflexibility of the self at the emotional level is not a sign of strength but of fragility and instability.

When our tallest buildings are constructed in areas subject to earthquakes, the deep footings are placed on rollers, allowing the building to flex with the stress which occurs during a quake. Rigidity is more susceptible to collapse under stress than flexibility. In the same way, emotional rigidity weakens the self's capacity to withstand stress.

In repressing emotion, the strongest emotion becomes fear that one will crack and that one's emotions will show. The repression of emotion thus causes a double bind. The more repression the more fear that repression will fail.

This is exactly the situation in which the man who came to me was caught. The fear that his emotions were out of control became part of the emotion which he was attempting to repress. He was caught in the myth that showing emotion was a sign of weakness. Deliverance from this fear begins by destroying the myth.

Myth #3: *Women are more emotional than men.*

The perception that women are more emotional by nature than men is also a cultural myth, based on the assumption that showing emotion is a sign of weakness. In a society that views emotional expression as a sign of weakness, and where males are expected to provide strong leadership and stability, men will be taught to suppress their emotions in order to be accepted.

Real men don't cry was the implicit rule in the society in which I grew up. The only tear I ever saw on my father's face was when he drove me to the train station the day I left for induction into the armed services at the age of eighteen. Not looking directly at me, he shook my hand, and with a quiver in his voice told me to take care of myself. Out of respect for his own sense of decorum, I pretended not to notice the tear and shed none of my own. Only now can I weep as I write this. What a tragic loss of those feelings unexpressed and unacknowledged! What a terrible price to pay for the myth equating emotion with weakness!

Once it is understood that likening weakness to emotional expression is a myth, it becomes apparent that the *lack* of emotional expression on the part of males is a mark of incapacity and weakness rather than strength!

Women *are* generally more emotionally expressive than men. But it is not due to a gender deficiency in women. The truth is, men are less emotionally expressive than women because they are socialized into this pattern from childhood. It is not that men do not have emotions, but that they are forced into suppressing them. They are as much the victims of the myth as are women.

This myth's power is devastating. Women are denied the self-affirmation and assurance that truly belongs to the strength and power of the self capable of emotional expression. Men are denied the very strength and power of the emotional life for the sake of a false self-perception and social acceptance. Liberation for both women and men can only come through the destruction of the myth.

Myth #4: Emotions are irrational.

Perhaps the most powerful myth concerning emotion is that it confuses and distorts reason. The origin of this myth lies with the concept that the mind is the basis for all rationality. In this view, emotions are considered to be subjective, while mental constructs are held to be objective and the basis for rational thought and action. When reason has been isolated from emotion it becomes abstract, impersonal, and predictable.

This is reflected in our choice of metaphors. "He was ruled by the heart and not the head," we say of someone who made what we might think was a foolish decision. We assume that the head is the seat of pure intellect and logic, while the heart is the source of feelings and emotions. According to the myth, pure intellect is rational while feelings are irrational. On the contrary, the emotional life is closer to the core of the self than is the mind.[1]

Reason is not a function of the intellect alone. The self's response to the full range of sensory experience begins with the feelings produced by sense perception—we become aware of persons and events through our five senses:

sight, hearing, touch, smell and taste.

If I am awakened in the night by a rumbling noise and a sensation of movement, certain feelings are aroused by these specific sense perceptions. There is an increase in adrenaline, my heart may beat faster, and I will have a feeling of apprehension and perhaps fear.

My first thought may be that there is an intruder in the room and that I am in danger. Fear moves up several notches and becomes stark terror! The thought that an intruder might be about to harm me causes initial feelings to become strong emotions of fear and terror. When the light is turned on, and there is no evidence of an intruder, other possibilities are now considered. Perhaps it was an earthquake. The radio is turned on and sure enough, there are already reports of an earthquake and some initial assessments of damage. This change in mental perception, from an intruder to an earthquake, changes the emotion from a fear of immediate attack to one of apprehension concerning another earthquake.

It would be irrational to insist that there is an intruder in the room when, in fact, there is none. But it is not irrational to have the feeling of fear in the face of the possible threat of an aftershock. Precautions can be taken to minimize damage should such an event occur. In other words, the emotion of fear is now based on a more accurate mental perception. As time passes without further aftershocks, the emotion of fear recedes.

Rationality is not the absence of emotion, but the appropriate kind and amount of emotion with respect to the reality of the world we experience through our sense perception.

It would also be irrational to deny the fear and repress the feelings produced by the experience. Rationality is thus a blend of feelings which are produced by sense experience and mental perceptions which accurately assess the facts so far as they can be ascertained. Sense experience and the feelings generated by the senses comprise an indispensable contact with reality and thus provide the core of rationality.

When the emotion of fear becomes separated from the original sense perception, it becomes a free-floating anxiety. The anxious feeling is no longer connected to what our senses tell us leading to reactions quite disproportionate to the reality of the situation we are in. Anxiety also stimulates our senses so that our body responds with the physiological reactions which ordinarily would be produced by the sense experience itself. The body prepares for action: Adrenaline is released, the heart pumps faster.

These responses, under some level of constant arousal due to anxiety, produce stress and cause the nervous system to be on constant alert. The body begins to send signals of overload, with physiological symptoms such as elevated blood pressure, chronic fatigue, or involuntary muscular movements. If the symptoms are treated through medication, temporary relief may result, but the underlying anxiety will not dissipate. Recovery from this kind of emotional distress involves tracing the anxiety back to the emotion of fear. Once we have moved from anxiety to fear, emotional health can be restored through a process of rerouting the emotion through the self's rational perception of one's environment and relational network in a realistic way.

The integration of the self and the development of emotional reason begins with the opening up of the emotional self to the reality of our relation to others, to our selves, and to God in whose image we are formed. We can break the power of the myth, says John Macmurray, by bringing the emotions, like Cinderella, out of the kitchen into the living area!

Emotion is not the Cinderella of our inner life, to be kept in her place among the cinders in the kitchen. Our emotional life is *us* in a way our intellectual life cannot be; in that it alone contains the motives from which our conduct springs.[2]

The recovery of emotional reason is an indispensable aspect of the rationality of living and loving. This occurs as we destroy the myth that emotions are irrational.

Myth #5: *Being emotional is to be out of control.*

The common view that emotion is irrational is kept alive from generation to generation by the myth that to express one's emotions is to lose control. When life is ordered by the laws of intellectual rigor and the straight lines of logic, emotion will always be viewed as a form of rational delinquency.

This is reinforced by legal definition when one category of homicide receives a lesser penalty due to it being a "crime of passion." Actions which are viewed as exceptions to the "normal" pattern of orderly and rational life are explained by "temporary insanity," of being aroused more by emotion than controlled by reason. This view of emotion places it outside of the control of the self and "passion" thus acquires a kind of fatalistic character. This is a secular version of the defense, "The devil made me do it!"

Emotion is not a "state of being" outside of our control. Perhaps, like some who blame the devil, the concept that emotions are essentially irrational and thus outside of our control, is part of our own defense mechanism. Having split emotion from reason, we treat our emotions like an untamed animal and try to keep them in a cage. When they break out, we can always argue that it is not in our power to control them. We are expected, however, to build a stronger cage for the sake of our neighbors.

When we put our emotions in a cage we repress the deepest feelings of the self. A chronic state of repression not organically caused may well be a sign that we have put our emotions in a cage and lost touch with our real feelings.

Recovery of emotional control is not an act of the will, but rather, freeing emotion to find its own boundaries within the self and its relationship with reality beyond the self. Healthy emotions are elastic and shaped. The shape of an emotion, such as fear or anger, is determined by the corresponding imprint of the particular sense experience which produces it. The emotion can also stretch to accommodate a wide range of feeling but return to its original shape when the intensity of the feeling is diminished.

Young people often have difficulty in maintaining a feeling within the shape or boundary of the appropriate emotion. When confronted with an experience of intense grief or sadness, for example, instead of allowing the emotion to stretch to accommodate the intensity of the feeling, an emotional "crossover" may occur and a nervous giggle may emerge.

Emotional growth occurs when each emotion develops its own configuration and when the emotion develops a wider range of feeling without distorting its shape. When emotions lose their shape or when they lose their elasticity, they appear to be irrational. Either there is little or no emotion, or the emotion is in a constant state of "flooding."

"Sometimes I feel that if I started crying I would never stop." The man who said this to me had no shape to his emotional life and little elasticity. He considered this to be an emotional weakness and sought to repress his feelings as the only way to prevent what he feared the most—a nervous breakdown.

Self-recovery for him meant the discovery of the emotional strength to handle the wide range of feelings which the self experiences in the course of a single day.

Like a "new wineskin," emotion must be elastic so that the proper shape will be formed in order to contain the "new wine" of an intense feeling without splitting. This metaphor, used by Jesus in his teaching, has relevance for the development of emotional health as well (Matt. 9:17).

Recovery of emotional health leads to recovery of emotional reason and effective emotional management. The beginning of this recovery process takes place when we destroy the myth that being emotional means being out of control.

Myth #6: Emotions are part of our personality.

"My husband is just a very angry person," his wife stated as a matter of fact. "His father was like that and I guess that he grew up to be just like him."

It was clear from the tone of her voice that she had become resigned to the fact that anger was part of her husband's personality and that he could never really change. One could hardly blame her for this perception. Emotional habits which become deeply entrenched seem to be embedded in the very core of our personality.

The fact is, emotions are *not* fixed elements of our personality which we cannot change. Far from being a deterministic factor of the human personality, emotions are capable of transformation and change. We should never feel that we are the victims of our emotions. Emotion represents the creative possibility of growth and change in the recovery of self.

Certainly there are facets of our personality which are beyond our control. Emotion, however, is not one of them.

While breaking emotional habits may be a difficult process, it is not impossible.

The beginning of recovery from damaging and destructive emotional habits is to destroy the myth that emotions are a fixed part of our personality. When our misunderstandings of emotion are revealed for the myths that they are, the positive work of recovering emotional health and strength can begin.

In examining our emotions and feelings, we have not yet found the core of the self. The source of emotional strength lies not in the passions, but in the spirit. It is the strength of the spirit which yields emotional health and strength. Self-recovery begins with locating our emotional center.

Locate Your Emotional Center

The human self has a spiritual core that is created in the image and likeness of God, who is Spirit and life. While our passions move us, it is spirit that gives the self direction and hope. If feelings are the core of emotion, spirit is the core and center of the self. Human feelings are not possible without spirit. Pleasure is an emotion based on feeling. Joy is a movement of spirit arising out of pleasure.[3]

"Emotion is inseparable from being filled with the spirit, which is above all a state of being moved," the Old Testament scholar, Abraham Heschel tells us. "Spirit implies the sense of sharing a supreme superindividual power, will or wisdom. In emotion, we are conscious of its being our emotion; in the state of being filled with spirit, we are conscious of joining, sharing or receiving 'spirit from above' (Isa. 32:15)."[4]

Emotions are personal and private. Even when expressed, they cannot really be shared. Sympathy says, "I know that you feel this way and I understand." Empathy says, "I have had that feeling too and am with you in your pain." There may be comfort in sympathy and consolation in empathy, but not inspiration.

It is instructive to remember that the biblical story of Creation depicts the formation of the first humans by saying, "The Lord God formed man from the dust of the ground, and breathed into his nostrils the breath of life; and the man became a living being" (Gen. 2:7). Human life is inspired life! To inspire is to "give spirit," to "quicken spirit." Following His death, the disciples of Jesus were inconsolable, though they each had similar emotions of discouragement and despair. Suddenly, they experienced Jesus Himself amidst them, and He "breathed on them and said to them, 'Receive the Holy Spirit'" (John 20:22). This inspiration gave rise to an emotional strength which empowered their lives to undertake incredible tasks, to endure incredible sufferings, and to experience incredible joy and hope.

The emotional center of the self is located in the spirit, not in the determinative events of the past nor in the capricious events of the present. The self has its source in Spirit, and therefore has a center which also points to a destiny. This is a center and destiny which cannot be molested nor violated. The inspiration of the Spirit of God guides us to self-recovery by placing the center of the self beyond the "slings and arrows of outrageous fortune," to use the language of Shakespeare. This is a spiritual orientation of the self which instructs the heart to "lay up treasure in heaven," to use the language of Jesus.

> "Do not store up for yourselves treasures on earth, where moth and rust consume and where thieves break in and steal; but store up for yourselves treasures in heaven, where neither moth nor rust consumes and

where thieves do not break in and steal. For where your
treasure is, there your heart will be also" (Matt. 6:19-21).

Take note. We are to lay up *for ourselves* treasures in
heaven; the desire for self-fulfillment is not itself an
unworthy emotion. There is need of a center for the self
which reaches back into the origins of the self within personal history and, at the same time, orients the contemporary self to a lodestar of future hope which shines its
brightness into the darkest of days.

> Today many people are longing for what now seems like
> an old-fashioned value, a cause, a goal, or an ideal that
> could be the lodestar of their lives. The emotional evi-
> dence of their predicament is their feeling of fragmenta-
> tion. Their emotions seem to be like echoes without origi-
> nal sounds. They lack a center: they have no direction.[5]

How can we discover and claim that center for ourselves
without being touched by the Spirit and stimulated by the
emotion which it summons forth within us? Our spirit is
the touchstone of that star, and our emotion the empowerment to pursue it. As Augustine said so many years ago,
"On our journey to God the affects are the feet that either
lead us closer to God or carry us farther from him; but
without them we cannot travel the way at all."[6]

CHAPTER THREE

Break Your Emotional Habits

"My husband is just a very angry person," his wife stated as a matter of fact. "His father was like that and I guess that he grew up to be just like him." When I told her that an emotion, like anger, is not part of our personality, but a learned habit that can be unlearned, she was openly skeptical. "He was that way before I married him and I thought that I could change him, but he will never change."

"Does he have any other bad habits," I asked, knowing that I would not be disappointed. "Well," she replied, with a hint of irritation in her voice, "I consider his anger more serious than a bad habit, but yes, he does. For example, he takes his shoes off when he is watching television and leaves them in the middle of the floor when he goes to bed. I have had to pick them up a hundred times. On several occasions I forgot and there they were when company came. I was so embarrassed."

Her momentary irritation at my question had now become a low grade anger at her husband!

"I wonder where he learned that habit," I probed. "Did he always do that?"

"Not in the beginning," she said, and then paused as if reconstructing an image in her mind. "As a matter of fact, when we were first married, I used to have him put his feet in my lap when he came home from work and I would give him a foot massage. I guess that was when he first started taking his shoes off in the family room."

"When did the foot massages stop?" I inquired innocently.

"When I began to work and we both came home about the same time. Often I would get home after he did. I guess we settled into a different pattern due to our work schedules. But I don't see why he can't learn to pick his shoes up! I tell him often enough but he just gets angry and lashes out at me."

Our emotions are clues to underlying patterns of the self's network of feelings which tend to produce habitual reactions and responses. The breaking of these emotional habits begins by listening to what our emotions tell us.

Listen to What Your Emotions are Saying

One of the oldest stories in the biblical tradition is found in the book of Genesis, where Cain and Abel, the two sons of Adam and Eve, present themselves to God, each with an offering (Genesis 4). God accepts the offering of Abel but not that of Cain. "So Cain was very angry and his countenance fell."

The first question asked of Cain by God was, "Why are you angry, and why has your countenance fallen?" God prompted Cain to listen to his emotions, to hear what his anger was saying about the inner disposition of his soul. As long as Cain allowed his anger to be directed toward an object outside of himself, he was not listening to what his anger was telling him about himself.

"Why am I angry?" he might have responded. "I am

angry because I feel devastated and miserable at the core of my very being. You have no idea what it feels like to have something you have carefully prepared rejected by the one to whom it is offered!" Well, that will do for a start!

"Tell me about it," God might have replied. And if Cain continued to express those deep feelings of rejection, hurt, and shame, he would have found a reason for his anger and discovered the place to begin the process of healing.

"Emotions signal something about the state of our well-being," says psychologist Mary Vander Goot. "Those which we experience as being desirable are those which signal that we are in a state that contributes to our good. Those which we experience as unpleasant are those which signal the need for a corrective. The signaling effect of emotion applies not only to our own well-being but also to the well-being of others."[1]

There is a wisdom hidden in our emotions, if we will only listen. Some of the messages which our emotions can reveal to us take us back to feelings which we have long since repressed or denied. We need to recover those feelings and reattach them to the living and growing self, making use of the emotional creativity at our disposal.

Feelings, of course, being related to sensations, are less amenable to change through thought. Feelings cannot be changed by thought because they originate in the self's response to sensation. Feelings can be transformed by the self through the development of new feelings. The life of the self is feeling—not a particular feeling, but the capacity to have feelings and to generate feelings.

Feelings which have become emotions, however, are susceptible to change as we access the emotion through the lens of perception. Emotions are flexible and fluid. We can move from an emotional high to an emotional low as quickly as the sun moves behind a cloud or a thought passes through the mind. Even where emotions have become habitual ways of perceiving the self, it is emotion that is most susceptible to change.

Reason receives its direction through emotion, and emotion receives its stimulation through feelings, for the self *is* its feelings. Feelings are generated by the stimulation of contact with the self's environment. The stimulation of other selves, therefore, affects one's emotions in a different way from any other encounter. It is through social interaction that the emotions of the self find expression beyond the feelings that produce them. When our emotions direct us to an authentic relationship with others and are validated in that relationship, then emotion becomes rational.

Emotion is created by thought brought out of a feeling. Anger is an emotion that is directed toward someone or something as a perceived cause of our feeling. The key to the emotion of anger is the accuracy of the perception that produces it. Breaking an emotional habit requires a change in the perception that formed the emotion.[2]

Self-recovery begins by seeking emotional health through emotional wisdom. Listening to what our emotions are telling us about our feelings is the beginning of that emotional wisdom.

Redraw Your Emotional Map

Emotional patterns are formed through a variety of perceptions, both conscious and unconscious. These patterns form what might be called our emotional map. Like a circuit board in the computer, our emotional map routes our feelings in configurations that produce "programmed" behavior or our emotional habits.

An emotional habit is like the anger of the man whose wife concluded that anger was a personality trait. His anger was predictable and pervasive, susceptible to being triggered by the slightest inconvenience or frustration. The anger was not directed so much at anyone as it was expressed as a normal reaction. Unfortunately it was felt by those around him as hostility and created distance and disturbance in the relationship. His anger had become so habitual that it assumed the status of a fixed temperament.

No longer could the anger be dealt with as a specific emotion. It was part of a greater emotional map of which he was quite oblivious. If he could acknowledge this pattern and be prepared to change, he would need to reroute his emotional map.

How was this map formed in the first place? Many of our emotional patterns are first formed through awareness prior to the development of language skills. Right brain functions tend to process sensory data through imaging and visualizing, while left brain functions process sensory data in a more conceptual and logical format. Right brain perceptions such as imaging stimulate emotions as much or more than logical and verbal cues. In this case, we acquire emotional patterns long before we create mental concepts of our experience through left brain activity.

Infants, we are told, are able to mimic facial expressions of adults during the first few weeks of their lives. Other forms of sensory experience are registered through visualization, hearing, smell, and touch. Once these feelings have become emotions they form a map by which the feelings are routed from perception to the core self. New feelings tend to follow the route formed by earlier ones, thus reinforcing the emotional patterns.

Later on, conceptual and verbal perceptions become attached to these emotions. Or rather, in some cases, the emotional pattern becomes attached to verbal and conceptual perceptions, interpreting them in ways consistent with the emotional map already formed.

For this reason, altering our perception as a way of changing emotional patterns does not only mean forming new mental concepts (left brain), but experiencing new awareness of self and one's environment (others) through creative imaging and visualization (right brain) techniques.[3]

Rerouting our emotional map might take the form of shifting from a left brain to a right brain mode of awareness.

If perception is considered a function of the entire brain operation, then imaging functions may be as useful in working with the emotions as are conceptual functions. This would be the case particularly where the formation of the emotion took place through a visual rather than a conceptual process. The self's experience through visualization and imagination opens up the emotional life to a creative perceptual function which works along with the conceptual function. This was a very important part of the function of memory and imagination for the Hebrew people, as John Pedersen makes clear.

> New and large experiences make one forget the lesser; they are displaced from the soul and exercise no influence. When the new heavens and the new earth are created, then the Israelites shall no more remember the former, and it shall not rise in their heart (Isa. 65:17; Jer. 3:16). It means that the new order of things shall fill their soul, so that the old no more stirs any emotion in it.[4]

The intentions of the heart, which express the same thing as we mean by the term "will," are connected to the concepts of the mind through the emotions. This is why attempts to change behavior by appealing directly to the mind through concepts usually fails. The creative dimension of the self is not isolated in mental activity but is a process of perception which includes emotion as well as intellect. Imagination, for example, as the power of visualizing something new, receives its stimulation through the emotions.

The man who has the habit of leaving his shoes in the middle of the floor is told repeatedly by his wife, "Tim, for goodness sakes, can't you learn to pick up your shoes?" The verbal communication has no effect on the emotional pattern which underlies the habit, except to trigger the emotion of anger! We remember that the removal of the shoes was accompanied originally by a highly sensual and stimulating feeling produced by the foot massage. The ritual of removing the shoes was accompanied by sensual stimulation. When the stimulation ended through a change in the relationship, the removal of the shoes continued as a habit. At the subconscious level, the removal of the shoes continued to massage the feelings of the self. The fact that habits fulfill subconscious needs for stimulation make them powerful and difficult to break.

The emotional map for this man has several direct access routes which connect emotion to action, each of which produces habitual behavior and reactions.

For example, the removal of the shoes continued to have an emotional effect lodged in the subconscious. Verbal communication alone did not access this emotion which underlay the habitual pattern. Rather, the verbal challenge, "Tim, for goodness sakes, can't you learn to pick up your shoes?" was picked up by quite a different route on his emotional map. As a child, he no doubt was told by his mother in somewhat the same tone of voice, "Tim, for goodness sakes, can't you learn to wipe your feet before you come into the house?" This verbal communication produced a feeling of guilt and probably shame, resulting in the emotion of anger aimed at his mother for making him feel this way.

In his case, the emotion of anger acquired a habitual pattern so that whenever he is made to feel shamed or humiliated, anger kicks in. In the shoes incident, we see both the verbal and nonverbal formation of the emotional map. Taking off the shoes is a learned emotional habit. It is a nonverbal cue to the subconscious feeling of a foot massage.

Anger expressed during a reprimand is also a learned emotional habit. It is a verbal cue activating a subconscious feeling of shame and triggering anger. The power of shame and the dynamics of recovery will be discussed further in Chapter Eleven.

The unlearning of the habits and the learning of new ones requires a rerouting of the emotional map by accessing the emotion involved through both verbal and nonverbal sense perception.

Take Responsibility for Your Emotional Habits

"Be angry but do not sin," counseled the Apostle Paul, "do not let the sun go down on your anger" (Eph. 4:26). Anger can become an emotional habit. Because it permits the self to project negative feelings on another, it serves well to protect us from deeper feelings of shame, hurt, and rejection. Taking responsibility for anger means neither denying this emotion nor repressing the feelings which gave rise to it. Rather, it means doing something to the anger instead of letting the anger do something to you and others.

Paul apparently felt that such often hurtful emotions could be self-managed if not transformed into more positive emotions. "Put away from you all bitterness and wrath and anger and wrangling and slander, together with all

malice, and be kind to one another, tenderhearted, forgiving one another, as God in Christ has forgiven you"
(Ephesians 4:31-32).

I don't think that Paul meant that we should vent our
emotions as a means of releasing them. Rather, the emotions which controlled such attitudes and behavior were to
be "put away." Paul does not tell us how this is to be done!
But it surely involves letting go of the negative emotions
by the creative process of forming new and more positive
ones. The practice of venting one's emotions in order to
gain freedom from them may not be helpful.[5]

Emotions, such as anger, jealousy, and fear, may rest on
incorrect perceptions. Changing these emotions involves
correcting the perception. If the perception is correct and
there is a real basis for the anger or fear, then one can deal
with the perception as reality and take appropriate action.

Rerouting our emotional maps requires two levels of
change in perception. At the conscious level, we can recal-
ibrate our thought process so that more accurate perceptions of reality can be attached to our feelings. When Tim
becomes aware that his habit of taking off his shoes and
leaving them in the middle of the floor is related to the
feelings he had when they were removed for the purpose of
having his feet massaged, he will begin to understand *why*
he continues to do this.

When he becomes aware of the fact that his anger at
being told to pick up his shoes has its source in an
unhealed sense of shame and a reaction directed against his
mother, he will begin to understand *why* he has this habitual anger.

The recalibration of these habits at the conscious level
alone, however, may not be sufficient to alter the pattern of
behavior. Because the habit of removing the shoes was
originally connected to a sensual stimulation, his wife may

discover a way of accessing his emotional map. This might be done by taking the shoes with one hand and her husband with the other and walking both back to the bedroom for the purpose of creating a stimulating sense experience which will alter his emotional map. Well, it was just an idea!

When we listen to what our emotions tell us, we move out of the blind rage of feelings into an understanding of why we feel and act a certain way. We can then begin to take responsibility for our emotional habits by tracing them to their roots. "Either make the tree good, and its fruit good; or make the tree bad, and its fruit bad; for the tree is known by its fruit" (Matt. 12:33).

Emotional habits which are formed through nonverbal sense experience may be broken more easily through imaging or visualization techniques than by mental concepts alone. If Tim is responsive to the suggestion that his emotional habit of anger can be broken, he may be guided through imagery to recover new feelings of self-worth as a way of altering his emotional map. When he begins to listen to what his emotional habit is telling him, he will be able to start the journey of self-recovery.

CHAPTER FOUR

Recover Your Positive Self-Esteem

"I'm not very happy with myself," Tim admitted. "My wife complains that I am always angry and impossible to live with. You call it an emotional habit that can be broken. But I must admit to you that I think it goes deeper than that. She will tell you that I got my angry personality from my father. What I really got was a feeling that I was just a stupid kid and could never do anything right."

"Do you still feel that way?" I asked.

"I don't understand it," he replied. "I'm quite successful in my work. I received an award just last year for designing a new merchandising plan for our company. I came home from that meeting expecting to get some appreciation from my wife and instead, got dumped on for not telling her about the award meeting. How do you figure that?"

"She made you feel stupid?"

"Maybe I am stupid to think that I could ever please her. What does it take to prove to someone that you're successful?"

Tim does not think that he has a problem with self-esteem. He will say that he sees himself as successful but that others do not appreciate him for what he is worth. At the same time, he admits that he is not happy with himself and can't escape the fact that he is still a "stupid kid" in his father's eyes. He needs to recover from the self-abuse of negative self-esteem.

What is Negative Self-Esteem?

Self-esteem is the valuing aspect of self-concept. Rather than referring to high or low self-esteem, I prefer the terms positive and negative self-esteem. A positive self-perception indicates a high degree of correspondence between one's self-perception and the "ideal" self. A negative self-perception suggests that the self fails to measure up to its own standard regardless of how that standard is set.[1]

Dr. Archibald Hart, Dean of the Graduate School of Psychology at Fuller Theological Seminary suggests that both low and high self-esteem may be unhealthy. "It is sufficient to stop hating yourself," he concludes. "For me a healthy attitude of the self toward the self is the absence of self-hate."[2]

Is self-hate too strong a term? Most of us do not like to think that we actually hate ourselves. At the same time, most of us would admit to times when we have said to ourselves, if not to others, "I hate myself when I do things like that." Even as we say it, we are probably using the words as a form of self-scolding. We really mean that we hate the things that we do. But the message seeps through to the core of the self and reinforces negative self-esteem.

Self-hate, whether we recognize it or not, may result from an unrealistic concept of the ideal or normative self as perceived by us or from the assessment of others. Regardless of how high a level of self-esteem is held by the self, if it falls short of a perception of what one ought to be it will result in negative self-worth.

Tim has negative self-esteem despite the fact that he perceives himself to be successful and even has an award to prove it. The negative aspect in his self-esteem is the contempt which he feels toward himself for not really being worthy of the success he has earned. He does not like himself very much when he becomes angry. In fact, he probably scolds himself afterward by saying, "I hate myself when I act like that."

This is what I call the "Willy Loman syndrome."

In his classic play, *The Death of a Salesman*, Arthur Miller traces, with unerring insight, the desperate unraveling of the dream for Willy Loman. Loman is a salesman whose self-image is unrealistically pinned to his dreams of success while denying the reality of his failures. The quiet desperation of Willy to succeed is projected onto his two sons, Biff and Happy who, at first, are captivated by the dream and then are forced to become accomplices in a charade.

At the end, unable to maintain the pretense, Willy precipitates a fatal accident while imagining himself a hero when the $20,000 insurance check arrives for his family. Following the funeral service, a postmortem on his life is conducted by Biff, who could no longer sustain the pretense. The other son, Happy, and Willy's friend, Charley, continue to defend Willy's self image.

BIFF: He had the wrong dreams. All, all, wrong.

HAPPY: Don't say that!

BIFF: He never knew who he was.

CHARLEY: Nobody dast blame this man. You don't understand; Willy was a salesman. And for a salesman, there is no rock bottom to the life. He don't put a bolt to a nut, he don't tell you the law or give you medicine. He's a man way out there in the blue, riding on a smile and a shoeshine. And when they start not smiling back—that's an earthquake. And then you get yourself a couple of spots on your hat, and you're finished. Nobody dast blame this man. A salesman is got to dream, boy. It comes with the territory.

BIFF: Charley, the man didn't know who he was.[3]

There is little agreement among psychologists as to just what constitutes self-esteem and less agreement as to what role it plays in a person's achievement of success and social adaptation. The Final Report of the California Task Force to Promote Self-Esteem, issued in 1990, found only anecdotal evidence that low self-esteem contributes to poor performance in school and leads to anti-social behavior. No direct causal connection could be established although there was a consensus that some correlation did in fact exist. Despite this ambivalence, raising self-esteem, the task force concluded, was one way to develop increased responsibility on the part of individuals for the general good of society.[4]

"The man didn't know who he was," said Biff Loman of his father. Willy Loman's self-perception was negative. For whatever reason, he despised himself and sought redemption in the only way left to his tormented mind. He concluded that he was worth more to his family dead than alive, and in his grandiosity, fed by despair, sought nobility through self-sacrifice.

The problem of negative self-esteem is often concealed in heroic efforts to compensate for self-hatred. This may be one reason why it is so difficult to establish a direct causality between self-esteem and social behavior. When society rewards success and associates self-image with role status and product identification, conformity to these ideals becomes a powerful stimulant. Self-esteem as a self- image is gained at the price of a feeling of self-worth.

When self-hatred wears the disguise of a victim, it becomes a family secret which can be passed from one generation to another like a genetic disease. Tim's father called him a stupid kid, probably to explain his own sense of failure as a parent. Tim assumed the role, but sought to prove his father wrong by attempting to find self-esteem in the eyes of others. The discrepancy between his unrealistic standard of self-esteem and his actual negative self-worth eats away at him like a hidden tapeworm.

Anger at being made to feel stupid is the disguise for self-hatred. Anger is the emotional defense of the victim, finding readily available targets in the theater of everyday work and living. In an attempt to defuse or deflect the anger, a wife and children may assume the roles of victim. "Stupidity," as one of my students once put it, "is a birth defect acquired from a dysfunctional family." This same student only began her recovery when she discovered that *feeling* stupid was a stupid way to live! She is now in the process of recovering her positive self-esteem.

Recover Your Positive Self-Esteem

Self-recovery begins with the recovery of positive self-esteem. This involves the recovery of three things:

- an original capacity for self-pleasure.

- an empowering experience of unconditional acceptance and love.

- an increased tolerance for delayed gratification.

1. The recovery of an original capacity for self-pleasure.

Jesus, the master teacher, once said, "Truly I tell you, unless you change and become like children, you will never enter the kingdom of Heaven" (Matt. 18:3). He thus implied that there is some essential goodness which the child possesses and which needs to be recovered. This childlike joy and happiness is the motivating source for self-fulfillment that is indispensable to faith, hope and love. The self-love which is typical of a child is a form of self-pleasure at its most elemental level.

When Jesus exhorted us to "receive the Kingdom of God as a little child," it is an encouragement to rediscover the longing which opens us up to God's love and the fulfillment of the self in another. It may well be that Jesus was reminding adults that they carry within them a childlike longing which, unfortunately, can become a childish bent toward controlling their own destiny and securing their own gratification through controlling others.

The love of God is an empowering love, aimed at evoking in each person the desire for the Kingdom of God and "everything else added to it" (Matt. 6:33). God's desire is to give us all things that pertain to life and happiness.

What I have called the capacity for "self-pleasure," psychologists sometimes refer to as narcissism. The psychotherapist William Meissner suggests that there is a "fundamental narcissism" which is essential to personal well-being in the adult. Experienced losses to this narcissistic core play a critical role in self development.[5]

There are religious traditions which claim that all children are born with original sin. These traditions often view the self as totally without value, with every aspect of the self corrupted and disposed toward wrongdoing. The redemption of the self, then, requires a replacement of this sinful self with a new self, based in the grace of God.[6]

I believe that it is a mistake to equate the innate capacity for self-pleasure with a sinful self-nature. It is much more helpful to identify the source of negative self-esteem in a distortion of self-pleasure rather than in self-pleasure itself.

I think that we would all agree that infants are born with a strong capacity for self-pleasure that looks very much like an unbridled instinct for self-gratification! We do not scold infants for this innate capacity for self-pleasure, but encourage and reward it. It is only when the infant grows into a child and then into an adult that this capacity for self-pleasure can become a source of others' irritation and disapproval. This capacity for self-pleasure, or narcissism, is not a negative attribute of the self. Rather, it is the positive basis for self-esteem.

The image of God with which each person is endowed is the source of positive self-worth and self-fulfillment. This is the infant's capacity to love itself, which I have called the capacity for self-pleasure. Behind self-pleasure is the deeper longing for self-fulfillment, which is one aspect of what we mean by the image of God. Self-fulfillment is the capacity for self-love in the most positive sense of valuing one's own life as a gift. This capacity is also the basis for the love of others, including God as the source of life.

For the infant, self-gratification and self-fulfillment are fused and experienced as the same feeling. When resistance is encountered to self-gratification the self feels powerless and threatened. This is where negative self-esteem has its beginning. When self-gratification is denied, it is experienced as a loss of power to control and fulfill one's own needs. The original capacity for self-pleasure which had a positive reward for the self, now experiences loss. Indeed, the expression of this capacity in the form of self-gratification brings disapproval, leading to feelings of a loss of self-worth.

When little Timmy seeks to fulfill his capacity for self-pleasure by taking away the toy from his older sister, he encounters resistance from his sister who violently takes back the toy! The caregiver who intervenes in the quarrel scolds Timmy for taking what is not his and he is sent to his room as punishment. Not only has the gratification of his self-pleasure capacity been frustrated, but he feels helpless.

When the child's expressed need for self-gratification is resisted by the caretaker, it is not only experienced as denial of pleasure but also as loss of power. This feeling of powerlessness at not being able to find immediate gratification from self-pleasure causes a variety of compensatory behaviors to kick in. The goal of these behaviors is to manipulate the source of gratification and produce a response. A new set of behavior patterns is quickly learned and reinforced by the caregiver's adaptation to the demands. The child is soon back in control of its environment and the core narcissistic needs are being fulfilled.

Timmy does not like to be made to feel bad when he is punished for attempting to gratify his own needs for pleasure. Nor does he like the feeling of being out of control. By throwing a temper tantrum he challenges the power of the caregiver and may succeed in gaining some attention, if not some compensation.

"How about some milk and cookies, Timmy," the exasperated caregiver may suggest. This diversionary tactic succeeds in separating the siblings and provides Timmy with a new pattern of behavior which leads to an alternative form of self-gratification. Power is a stimulant to which one can become addicted in early childhood! In fact, as we shall see later on in this book, the source of much addictive behavior lies in the gratification it produces for unfulfilled self-pleasure.

In Timmy's case, the capacity for self-pleasure has become confused with the need for power and control as the provider of self-gratification. This is the point at which many identify original sin with the self, so that all attempts to speak of the intrinsic worth of the self in terms of the longing for pleasure and self-fulfillment are labeled sinful. This is the point where narcissism becomes associated with self-gratification rather than with self-fulfillment.

This confusion between self-fulfillment and self-gratification is important and yet so subtle that it is often overlooked in the discussion of self-esteem. Those who judge any attempt to speak of self-esteem as humanistic and unbiblical fail to see the image of God as the very core of the self. Those who encourage the development of positive self-esteem as the way to emotional health and a successful life may fail to see the need to liberate self-esteem from self-gratification and its power mechanisms.

There is an assumption common to certain religious traditions that feelings of self-worth and concern for self-esteem are inappropriate at best and unspiritual at worst. For many in this tradition, the self is to be viewed as hopelessly enslaved and utterly worthless. They like to quote the apostle Paul (out of context!) who said, "For I know that nothing good dwells within. . . ." (Rom. 7:18).

What they neglect to mention is Paul's positive affirmation in the same context: " . . . I delight in the law of God in my inmost self" (Rom. 7:22). This inward delight in God remained for Paul the positive core of his self-worth and the basis for his recovery and growth.

The image of God and the concept of sin must be differentiated clearly so that the core of the self is not *essentially* destroyed by sin. This is important for psychological reasons as well as religious. The psychology of self-identity requires a thread of continuity through even the most severe forms of mental illness and emotional disorder. A healthy religious concept of self-identity likewise requires continuity through the radical experience of new birth and spiritual renewal.

Religion has tended to be more concerned with the eradication of sin and the implanting of a "new nature" than with the preserving of self. Psychology has tended to be more concerned with restoring the self than with providing a "new nature" through the empowering gift of the grace of God.

The key to healthy recovery of the original capacity for self-pleasure is a source of empowerment which supports and fulfills the self through the process of delayed gratification. Delayed gratification is always experienced as a loss of control and power to fulfill one's own needs. Deeper than any need for gratification, however, is the longing for self-fulfillment. To be empowered to realize self-fulfillment beyond the gratification of needs is to receive the grace of God.

The second phase of the recovery of positive self-esteem provides for an empowering experience of unconditional acceptance and love through which the original capacity for self-pleasure and self-fulfillment can be restored in a healthy way.

2. An empowering experience of unconditional acceptance and love.

The initial utterance of Adam upon encountering Eve, so the Bible tells us, was, "This at last is bone of my bones and flesh of my flesh; . . . " (Gen. 2:23). Should we not be surprised at this? Were we not expecting something a bit more—well, relational if not romantic? Granted, Adam had a tender place in his side and a piece of rib cartilage missing. The prompting of physical sensation has a way of prioritizing our feelings!

But we may have missed the clue to the extraordinary discovery which lies behind the utterance. For the first time, Adam utters the personal pronoun, "my." Here at last, Adam cries out, is one who is "of my bones and . . . my flesh." We forgive him this initial preoccupation with his own self-recognition and self-perception. Up to this time he has not only been "alone" but without a perception of his own self as different from and yet united to another.

The dawning of self-perception appears in the encounter with another self. This is a healing encounter, for it is one which creates wholeness out of what had only been a part. We must not pass too quickly over this important moment. The emergence of the self does not occur by transcending the "flesh and bones," of our physical existence, but through the encounter of the self of the other through one's own embodied existence.

The biblical concept of the image of God is grounded in the experience of the self with others. While each person is fully endowed with the image of God, this divine image is experienced in the self's encounter with others. In this depiction of the formation of the first humans, there is an empowerment to discover and experience being one with and through the other.

Martin Buber, the Jewish philosopher most remembered for his classic treatise on the nature of the self as personal and relational wrote:

> The You encounters me by grace—it cannot be found by seeking. But that I speak the basic word to it is a deed of my whole being, is my essential deed. . . . The basic

word I-You can be spoken only with one's whole being. The concentration and fusion into a whole being can never be accomplished by me, can never be accomplished without me. I require a You to become: being I, I say you.[7]

The other person provides the necessary boundary for the self to be experienced in a relation of mutual trust and acceptance. When we give priority to self-reflection and self-consciousness in abstraction from relation to the other, our movements toward others will be cautious and even mistrustful. "I need you to be myself," says John Macmurray.

This need is for a fully positive personal relation in which, because we trust one another, we can think and feel and act together. Only in such a relation can we really be ourselves. If we quarrel, each of us withdraws from the other into himself, and the trust is replaced by fear. We can no longer be ourselves in relation to one another. We are in conflict, and each of us loses his freedom and must act under constraint.[8]

The importance of social interaction in the differentiation of the self is a direct result of the image of God in relation to others rather than to the self alone. The awakening of the infant to selfhood and the beginning of the development of the image of God as a possibility and personal history of fulfillment is linked to its encounter with others. This begins at the earliest point of the infant's life; the face that shines upon the infant in love reflects and mediates the love and grace of God.[9]

Let me review what has been said. The longing for self-fulfillment must be rescued from its enslavement to the instinct for self-gratification. When this longing becomes a need, we will use whatever power we can find at our disposal to fulfill it. This is the psychological basis for the religious category of sin. It is a violation of the image of God and is the root of self-destructive behavior as well as violence against others.

The self becomes powerless when it seeks to gratify its own needs and fulfill its own longings. Paradoxically, this sense of powerlessness becomes a powerful drive to gratify the self's needs. Recovery of the original longing for self-fulfillment can only occur through an encounter with others where unconditional love and acceptance is experienced. This is what is called in religious terminology, grace. God is the ultimate source of this grace, though it is often mediated and experienced through relations with others.

Where do we find this unconditional acceptance and love?

We find it with people who have themselves begun the process of self-recovery. Here are the characteristics of such people:

- An admission of one's own need for healing and help in the pilgrimage toward personal well-being
- An acceptance of the care and support of others with no attempt to exploit them for personal gratification
- A commitment to honesty in self-assessment coupled with a gracious intolerance of dishonesty and deception in the assessment others have of themselves
- A capacity to accept others with no strings attached and sustain unconditional commitment to their well-being and growth
- A freedom to acknowledge and express gratitude for the source of divine grace as personal empowerment for growth.

3. An increased tolerance for delayed gratification

The single test for self-empowerment and recovery is the tolerance for delayed gratification. This tolerance lies beyond the capacity to realize the three great virtues of the fulfilled life—faith, hope, and love (1 Cor. 13:13).

Tolerance for delayed gratification is a measure of the freedom of the self to realize self-fulfillment beyond the gratification of needs.

At the age of twenty months, my grandson Brandon had what I considered to be his fair share of toys. As I observed him playing outside with neighborhood children, there appeared to be a fair balance within that general age group. But as I watched them happily playing, it soon became apparent that pleasure is a fragile experience in the toyland of childhood.

It was the yellow car in which Thomas sat that captured the imagination of Brandon. Walking right up to it, he attempted to push Thomas out and crawl in himself. The consternation in the face of Thomas was only exceeded by the bright-eyed zeal in the eyes of Brandon who, despite being outpointed in months and size, sought to take physical ownership of what had already become his by desire. The result? Two unhappy little boys. One denied access to a toy he truly needed to be happy; the other desperately gripping the steering wheel of a car that was now secured with fear and trembling.

The fun had gone out of the toy. It was now a possession to be defended against the unprovoked terrorism of his little friend. Would he ever again be able to play happily with his little yellow car without a sense of fear that he could lose it in a moment to his closest playmate? And how about Brandon? Would his stable of toys be sufficient now that he had been denied the one thing on which his heart was set?

The fact that a few hours later both boys were happily playing together (the yellow car had been confiscated by parental discretion), reminds us of how quickly happiness can be restored when the attention span is short! And yet, one suspects that a lesson had been learned—someone else always has more toys! This is the first lesson of childhood unhappiness. Life is not fair. What your heart desires, your hands cannot acquire. What is rightfully yours can be lost to another.

When that which is deemed necessary for one's pleasure is denied, either by confiscation or negation, it is not experienced as delayed gratification of pleasure, but as a violation of one's right of ownership. When the yellow car is confiscated, both Brandon and Thomas are offended, each in their own way. No compromise can be accepted and no promise of future pleasure will suffice. For the immediate sensation is not only loss of pleasure, but outrage over a violation of what each feels is rightfully theirs.

In some cases, children can be coaxed out of their temper tantrums by an immediate offer of an even greater gratification—a double dip ice cream cone, for instance. This, however, only compounds the problem. The use of pleasure to alleviate a sense of moral outrage is a quick fix of happiness, leaving the underlying unhappiness unhealed and untouched. There is a deeper longing which remains unfulfilled. Later in this book I will show how this "primitive moral" instinct, when frustrated, can lead to abusive relationships and even to violence.

Tolerance for delayed gratification is the mark of growth and maturity resulting in qualities of life which lead to *shalom*—the Hebrew word for peace—health, wholeness, and reconciliation.

The recovery of the image of God as the intrinsic value of the original self, resulting in positive self-esteem as empowerment for feelings of self-worth, has its source in divine love and grace. The empowering reality of divine grace does not annihilate the self but liberates it from the compulsion to find self-fulfillment through self-gratification. The capacity for self-pleasure of which I spoke earlier is thus preserved as the positive motivation of the self toward faith, hope, and love.

With the intervention of the grace of God the capacity for self-pleasure (narcissism) is freed from the need to control and is empowered by love to experience self-worth. The intervention of divine grace may be seen as providing empowerment for the self to retain the original capacity for self-pleasure in the form of self-worth or self-esteem. Delayed gratification is the evidence of this recovery which the apostle Paul calls the "fruit of the Spirit." These are: "love, joy peace, patience, kindness, generosity, faithfulness, gentleness, and self-control" (Galatians 5:22).

This is *spiritual* fruit because it is empowered by the Spirit of God. It is spiritual *fruit* because it is the result of the health and growth of the self as a human self grounded in the image of God. The integration of psychological concerns for health and wholeness coincide with religious concerns for a spirituality which is also the recovery of the true humanity of the self. In the same way, religious concerns for the effects of sin arising out of the self merge with psychological concerns for dysfunctional and disruptive behavior at the personal and social level.

Going back to the earlier example, through his anger Tim has learned to gratify a need that is never satisfied. It is the need to compensate for his own lack of self-worth and to disguise the bottomless pit of self-hatred. As long as the expression of anger offers him greater reward than the repression of it, he will feel compelled to use that tactic.

Tim needs to discover the reward and self-fulfillment that can come through a self-love and self-worth that finds pleasure in contributing to the good of others. Empowerment rather than condemnation and punishment is the secret to self-understanding. Tim is out looking for the kind of people who will provide that empowerment. He has taken the first steps toward recovery.

PART TWO

SELF-CARE

The Movement Toward Healing and Hope

CHAPTER FIVE

If It Hurts, You Have Been Wounded

I was in my teens, as I remember the incident, sitting on the edge of the family circle nursing some grievance, the source of which escapes me now. When someone commented on my lack of participation, my mother responded, "Don't mind Ray, he's just got his feelings hurt!"

As I recall, the remark did not have a therapeutic effect! It was a common enough expression in those days, and I suppose that suffering over hurt feelings was thought to be like the common cold—there was no cure for it, but we were expected to get over it in a few days.

In retrospect, the reference to hurt feelings is a curious expression. What are feelings and how can they be hurt? One feels pain when injured, and we say "it hurts" when the doctor applies pressure to a sore spot on the body. The days of our childhood are filled with flurries of feelings, most of which seem to disappear without a trace, like a frown which suffers a meltdown in the face of a smile. But there are feelings in every child, that hurt beyond telling and these painful feelings become the strand on which the pearls of memory are strung. Some of these pearls of memory are misshapen and ugly. We may attempt to remove them or to heal them, but until the strand of hurt feelings itself is repaired, we are not on the journey to recovery.

When my feelings are hurt, I hurt from the inside out. There is no scrape on the knee or cut on the finger to which I can point when someone says, "Let me kiss it and make it feel better!" When my feelings are hurt I know that no one else in all the world feels as badly as I do. I feel the cut, the stab, and the stinging pain. The throb of hurt feelings is impervious to the analgesic remedies offered by well-meaning persons who seek to cheer us up!

"Just leave him alone," they say, when we won't dance at their party or join their parade. "He'll join us when he feels like it." They don't realize that if we have been hurt, injury has been done to us. We have been wounded. We can't just forget about it. We feel violated. Our hurt is laced with moral feelings.

Some Injuries Do Not Heal by Themselves

There are some injuries which heal with time. These can be painful but need not be permanent. Recovery from injuries produced by violation of our deepest feelings by another require moral retribution in addition to emotional repair. These are injuries to the self which are experienced as violations of one's personal possessions, space, and dignity or, in some cases, physical abuse. When these kind of injuries occur to children, the hurt may be carried into adulthood.

Recognition of the moral violation incurred in these type of injuries to the self is necessary to self-recovery and healing. In this chapter we will discover the deeper moral issue involved in the violation of the self and suggest strategies for recovery and healing.

The capacity for self-pleasure, as I have indicated earlier, is an indispensable and necessary aspect of the self. When this capacity is damaged or injured, by whatever means, it is experienced as a violation of the self's innate rights and not merely as deprivation of pleasure. Some psychologists speak of damage to the capacity for self-pleasure as "narcissistic injury." The resulting inability to experience true self-pleasure can produce compulsive and addictive behavior, in this view.

I believe that the injury suffered to the capacity for self-pleasure is also a violation of an innate moral aspect of the self. For the child, the earliest experience of denial toward self-pleasure is experienced as a violation of something which rightfully belongs to the self. This violation is what I mean by the phrase, "moral outrage." It is experienced by every person to some degree whenever the capacity for self-pleasure is frustrated or denied.

When small children become involved in conflict over possession of a toy, and one bites or pulls the hair of the other when robbed of the toy, we witness what I have called moral outrage in a very primitive form. When a child feels violated, the typical reaction is to resort to some form of violence against the offender. What lies concealed in this reaction is the deeper moral injury done to the one whose toy was taken, or whose personal sense of self was violated.

Children, of course, have not yet developed a category of moral discrimination. Their actions, while not expressed in moral terms, are grounded in a sense of moral outrage. This moral outrage is often blind and out of control. Nonetheless, it is an expression of a wounded self.

When an offense against us causes a sense of personal

violation, the feeling can be one of moral outrage. The expression of this feeling may take the form of anger. The anger can act as a defense of the vulnerable self that has been wounded. To berate persons for that anger and attempt to move them quickly to a position of passivity and acceptance is to deny them their feeling of having been violated, and leave them weak and even more vulnerable.[1]

Only when the sense of moral outrage is dealt with can the feelings of anger subside so that forgiveness can be offered and received. To force a child prematurely to say, "I am sorry," compounds the feelings of moral outrage. One cannot really feel sorry for anger which is an expression of moral outrage.

Why Some Injuries Produce Moral Outrage

When Jeff came to me for pastoral counseling his complaint was that he had an unresolved problem with his father which was seriously affecting his ability to concentrate on his studies. He was a doctoral student at a nearby university. His doctoral research was in the area of family systems theory, and part of his assignment was to develop a comprehensive family genogram. This involved interviewing all of his immediate family members and identifying the role of each person in his own family of origin.

As it turned out, he was a victim of sexual abuse by his father from the age of 8 through 13 years. The abuse stopped when his father divorced his mother and he lived with his mother and her brother through his high school years. He had never confronted his father with this abuse, although his mother had acknowledged her awareness of it and recommended it should be forgotten.

During his research, he had confronted his father with this fact. His father denied it and became very angry, accusing him of attempting to destroy his reputation and his relationship with his second wife.

"How can I recover from the damage done to me by my father if he will not acknowledge what he did? I cannot just pretend that it never happened. The other members of my family are now angry at me for causing such an upheaval over something that happened so many years ago. Am I being vindictive in attempting to get him to face up to what he did?"

"Are you angry at what he did to you then or at his refusal to accept responsibility for it now?" I asked.

"How can I tell?" he responded. It was not really a question. "I never really felt angry about it until now. I just felt shamed. I have always thought that I must have encouraged it or he would have stopped. I understand now that he was a very sick person to do that and that I was a helpless victim. But I still feel a sense of shame in talking about it. And my anger is so strong that it is destroying me."

As we probed his feelings of anger over a period of time, Jeff began to use words like, "I feel so violated." "I feel that he should pay for what he has done." "Why should he be allowed to live as if he has done nothing wrong?"

These phrases revealed an underlying sense of moral outrage. Jeff was not only physically abused, he was violated in the most profound moral sense of the word.

An adolescent boy has no criteria by which he can become the moral judge of his own father. Those moral feelings of outrage had to be suppressed under a blanket of shame. The injury incurred went far deeper than emotional pain. Moral wounds to the self do not heal, they must be expressed, acknowledged, and authenticated.

When violations of the moral integrity of the self occur through abusive relationships with others, the injury suffered produces an outrage which can only be healed through a process of moral clarification. This involves recovery of the feelings of moral outrage and assignment of moral judgment against the offender. This is particularly difficult when the injury to the self occurred through the actions of one on whom the self was dependent for emotional and physical care and support.

The psychotherapist William Meissner says, "We violate children and arouse them to an inner rage when we keep them from the guidance and support they need to develop fully." This violation of the self produces a reaction which he calls a primitive level of moral development. The feeling of being shamed, abandoned, or deprived of self-pleasure, lies behind the emotion of anger and can lead to violence as an expression of the moral outrage. These feelings of moral outrage can often lead to domestic violence. "There is a violence inherent in the moral sense," says Meissner.[2] I will discuss the relation of domestic violence and abuse to this primitive moral instinct later in the book.

The anger which Jeff now feels against his father is an expression of the moral outrage which he experienced as a child. Feelings are timeless in the sense that they are not lodged in events but in the core of the self. We plot incidents and events on a chronological continuum of past, present, and future. Feelings which are caused by incidents which occur in time become detached from this time sequence and are carried by the self in a timeless time capsule.

Feelings may be repressed but not forgotten. We can block the incident from our memory but we cannot erase the feeling it aroused in the self. This is why we are so often troubled by feelings that are experienced as keenly as when first aroused, but which have become detached from the original incident or event in our minds.

Feelings which have been repressed do not gradually

disappear or diminish. When the incidents which we have blocked from our memory reappear, as in the case with Jeff, the original feelings are revived. Jeff's anger is not only against his father's denial of the earlier incidents of abuse, but is fueled by the feelings of moral outrage which he experienced throughout the abuse, but which were denied expression.

How can a child act as the moral judge of his own care-giver? The child is faced with a terrible dilemma. Dependent on the caregiver for physical as well as emotional support, the child represses these feelings of outrage in order to receive affection and support in other areas. The child is caught in a double bind. The person from whom the child receives the care necessary to survive also inflicts upon the child psychological and moral torment. The feelings of outrage are split off and buried deep within the self. This enables the mind to block out the incidents from recall, leaving blank spaces in the adult's later memory of those years.

As an adult, Jeff now recalls the incidents and experiences the feelings as sharply and intensely as when first produced by the abusive incidents. The feeling of violation can now be acknowledged and must be dealt with as a moral issue which demands justice.

Turn Moral Outrage into Moral Health

Once moral outrage has been aroused, a moral verdict must be rendered. "It's not fair," a child will protest, when told that the trip to the amusement park has been called off. "You promised!"

"I know I promised," the parent responds patiently, "but daddy has to work this weekend and we will have to go another time."

The parent has a good reason. Very few promises in life are unconditional. For the child, however, the moral outrage continues unabated. No verdict can be rendered which will prove satisfactory to the child. For all of the protest, accompanied by coercive tactics learned in other disputes, the child will lose this one.

Failing to win a verdict which will appease the feeling of moral injustice, the child will often resort to punishment of the offending parent. Perhaps the parent can be made to feel guilty for failing to follow through on the promise. A prominent display of hurt feelings and a calculated period of sulking should arouse feelings of guilt in the parent, if not sympathy.

Without realizing it, the family room becomes a courtroom where parents are put on trial by their offspring! When the punishment has been sufficient, the child withdraws the complaint and justice has been served. Until next time!

In Jeff's case, the injury done to him by his father's abuse was so deep and pervasive that the moral outrage it caused remained hidden and repressed. Lacking the resources and support to mount a moral verdict against his father, Jeff turned the judgment upon himself and felt shame rather than outrage. Unable to think of his father as an evil person, he thought of himself as a bad person. Shame is self-inflicted punishment for a perceived moral failure.

The process of recovery began with the moral clarification of his anger. When he was allowed to express his anger as moral outrage against his father for the abuse, a verdict was now possible. His case was finally being brought to trial. I encouraged him to present his case as though he were the prosecuting attorney with the understanding that a verdict would be rendered.

It was a painful process. It was not easy for him to recall the specific occasions of the abuse. Details were lacking, though incidents and feelings were recoverable. He wrote out his indictment. It was almost more than he could bear. His emotions were like a roller coaster. More than once he was tempted to turn back from this exercise as too painful.

In the end, he made his case and I could affirm the verdict. His father was guilty as charged.

"But my father continues to deny it," he protested. "How can this be resolved as long as he will not admit that what he did was wrong?"

"Does his denial mean that he is not guilty?"

"I guess not," Jeff responded. "But I thought that I could only be healed through some kind of reconciliation with him. That's not going to happen."

This was the crucial point in his journey to recovery. Jeff wanted his father to confess and assume responsibility as a way of making up for the injury caused. When we have been violated by another, we want the other to suffer too as a kind of retribution. We expect the one who has abused and shamed us to remove the shame and make right the wrong. But this is impossible. This leaves the other with the power to continue the abuse, however, by resisting admission of guilt. Jeff did not want reconciliation as much as he wanted to punish his father as a way of removing the stigma and stain from his own life.

The need to punish an offender in order to satisfy moral outrage is a common feeling. But it is not the way to recovery. The moral demand is for a verdict, a judgment against the offender which satisfies the moral self. This verdict is rendered based on the facts and is supported by the moral wisdom of others who provide an objective point of reference. As in any court of law, the verdict rendered does not depend upon an admission of guilt but upon the weight of evidence submitted.

Moral injuries to the self are not healed the same as other injuries. Rather, these injuries must be treated as violations of one's innate sense of moral dignity and personhood. Recovery begins when a moral verdict is rendered in one's favor. This is impossible for the morally wounded self to do alone. The recovery of moral health results from the disclosure of the moral abuse and the discovery of moral empowerment.

The disclosure of moral abuse as the basis of moral outrage requires moral support. This requires sensitivity to the injury sustained through a violation of the self's innate dignity of personhood. A perception of moral injury is an insight beyond that of a diagnosis of emotional pain. With this insight, the one who provides moral support and clarification leads the injured one through a process resulting in a moral judgment against the offender. This process uncovers the source of the moral outrage and directs the moral judgment away from the victim toward the offender. This is the process which enabled Jeff to release his moral outrage against his father for the abuse he suffered as a child.

The discovery of moral empowerment is a second phase of the recovery process. Moral outrage which fails to be expressed honestly and accurately against the offender is deflected back upon the victim as shame and self-condemnation. Shame is a loss of moral worth and power. The power of shame is secrecy. As long as we keep the secret of our violation and abuse to ourselves, we feel safe and protected. The power of shame is only broken when we are empowered by a new sense of moral and personal worth. When Jeff began to experience the moral freedom to judge his father's actions as wrong, he discovered the moral depths of his outrage.

Moral outrage, after all, is a moral expression of the self. When it is repressed, the moral core becomes split off and turns an accusing eye upon the self, producing shame and self-condemnation. When moral outrage is expressed as anger it becomes destructive and even violent. The discovery of moral empowerment results from the discovery of the true moral self as endowed with the divine image and likeness.

The biblical story of Adam and Eve reveals the source of moral empowerment as they are confronted by their Creator following their fall from grace (Gen. 2 and 3). Led astray by the serpent, who covered his evil intention with the pretense of good, Adam and Eve lost their innocent and trusting relationship with each other. They now felt shame and self-condemnation. They covered themselves with fig leaves and hid themselves in the garden from the presence of God.

Confronted by God, they complain that they were tricked by the serpent, an acknowledgment of their own failure as much as an indictment of the evil one. At this point, we are surprised. The first judgment of God is against the serpent, who is brought under a curse for leading astray two of God's children. Two things then take place with regard to Adam and Eve. They are forced to lay aside the fig leaves which covers their shame, and then are clothed by God with the skins of animals.

These are powerful metaphors. As God's children, Adam and Eve are endowed with the divine image and likeness which is an innate sense of moral worth and value. As they are open and supportive of each other's integrity and worth, the story says that they were "both naked, and were not ashamed." When they experience the violation of that inner sense of value through the misleading guidance of the serpent, there is no open expression of moral outrage. Rather, this outrage is deflected back upon themselves and the moral injury they receive drives them into secrecy.

With the skill of a moral surgeon, God uncovers their sense of shame and moral confusion. There is no curse directed at the couple. Rather, the serpent receives the full force of the divine moral outrage as the one who has seduced and violated the children. While there are consequences of their actions which each must accept, the moral outrage of God turns into moral empowerment. They receive more than mercy. The metaphor of clothing which God provides is a gracious sign that they are accepted and valued as the children of God that they essentially are.

Did the serpent ever confess and acknowledge his moral crime against God's children? Never! But the verdict has been rendered. God serves notice. His moral outrage is the source of divine compassion and mercy directed toward those who bear his image, and the source of judgment and retribution toward those who violate that human image and likeness.

Central to the biblical story and the Judeo-Christian tradition is the reality of God as the defender of the defenseless and one who hears the cries of the oppressed. When we understand that each person has been endowed with the image and likeness of God, we can hear the outrage of those who are violated as an expression of a divine moral outrage. The God of Israel is a God who takes up the cause of those who have suffered at the hands of others and who asserts the moral worth and value of those who have suffered moral injustice.

While the prophets pronounce judgment against those who oppress others and fail to show mercy and love, their underlying theme is the moral verdict which God renders on behalf of those who have become victims.

> Justice is turned back, and righteousness stands at a distance; for truth stumbles in the public square, and uprightness cannot enter. Truth is lacking, and whoever turns from evil is despoiled. The Lord saw it, and it displeased him that there was no justice. He saw that there was no one, and was appalled that there was no one to intervene; so his own arm brought him victory and his righteousness upheld him. (Isaiah 59:14-16)

Jesus issued a stern warning against those who violate the moral dignity and value of those whom God cares for. "Take care that you do not despise one of these little ones; for, I tell you, in heaven their angels continually see the face of my Father in heaven" (Matt. 18:10).

But where do we really find the ultimate source of empowerment when our moral selves have been wounded and we need a moral verdict rendered on our behalf rather than moral judgment? To whom can we turn when we feel forsaken and abandoned, without a moral advocate and devastated by our own sense of failure and shame?

For many, the religious community provides a source of empowering love, including priests and pastors who mediate the grace and healing power of God. Therapists and counselors provide psychological assistance for the process of healing and recovery of emotional and mental health. Recovery groups and twelve-step programs offer a process and context of healing and growth. The beginning step of authentic recovery is the moral and spiritual empowerment that only God can give.

Recovery does not come through the healing of emotional pain alone. True recovery means the discovery of one's own moral and spiritual self as affirmed by God and empowered through divine love and grace.

In Heaven, Jesus told us, there are angels whose sole responsibility is to represent our case before the Father's face. When angels look down upon our faces, we feel blessed. When angels look into the face of God on our behalf, we have moral and spiritual power invested for our recovery. Listen to your angel!

CHAPTER SIX

If You Can't Stop Hurting, You Are Hurting Yourself

Meantime I seek no sympathies nor need-
The thorns which I have reaped
    Are of the tree I planted.
They have torn me, and I bleed.
I should have known what fruit
    Would spring from such a seed.

Lord Byron

The story was a tragic one. The newspaper account presented the facts as well as drawing out the human drama resulting from the death of an eighteen-year-old woman killed by a car driven by a young man who was under the influence of alcohol. A common enough tragedy, and one that happens all too frequently in most of our major cities. What gave this story its unique twist was the punishment devised by the girl's father and mandated by the court.

The girl was killed on a Friday. At the age of eighteen she had lived 216 months, according to the father's reckoning. The punishment recommended to the court was a fine of exactly $216, to be paid by a personal check for the amount of one dollar, written out in the girl's name, on Friday of each week for 216 weeks. The check was to be mailed by the young man to the girl's father each week. The court accepted the stipulation and set the fine accordingly. The man was released and ordered to pay his fine according to the schedule.

Two years have gone by, and the young man has been cited for contempt of court for not keeping up the payment schedule. He pleads for mercy from the judge. "I would gladly pay the total amount of the fine. In fact, I have written out a check to make the payment in full, but her father refused to accept it. He said that he wants me to write out a check each week so that I will not forget what I did to his daughter. I simply can't do it. It is killing me. I want to put this behind me."

The father is adamant and tells the court. "This man took eighteen years of my daughter's life. I am only asking that for every month that she lived he think once a week on his foolish disregard for her life. After all, he continues to live while my daughter is dead."

The court, according to the story, refused to change the terms of the penalty and required the young man to continue the weekly payments.

Which one is being hurt the most by this drawn out punishment, the father of the girl or the young man who was responsible for her death? The young man does not deny his responsibility, he only asks that he be allowed to pay the fine and put the incident behind him. He feels deep remorse for what he did, but finds no healing for his pain in the weekly reminder.

The father feels that some atonement needs to be made for the senseless loss of his daughter. He wants her name and memory to be kept alive for as many weeks as she lived. He does not feel that his request is unreasonable. After all, he says, the amount of money is not what is important, but the significance of his daughter's life.

In reading the story, one feels that both have become victims, each in their own way, of hurts that have not been allowed to heal. The father can't stop hurting nor does he want the young man who killed his daughter to get off without suffering as well.

The pain of this tragedy, acted out in a public courtroom, is played out daily in the lives of many of us. Having suffered an initial hurt, we require token payments of pain at regular intervals to keep the injury alive. This kind of pain issuing from an old hurt, strangely, can become like a craving for sweets. It requires regular feeding and is never satisfied.

As a woman told me who was going through a process of recovery from an abusive family and a hurtful marriage, "I thought pain was normal, and I felt empty and unsatisfied if I did not have some. It has taken me some time to discover that being without emotional pain is okay."

When You Can't Stop Hurting

There are some injuries which do not heal with time. These are injuries which are laced with moral feelings. In the previous chapter I talked about these kind of injuries. Any perceived violation of the self's innate sense of dignity and personhood produces a kind of moral outrage. Injuries to the self which result in moral outrage require a verdict which satisfies our inner sense of moral justice, primitive and blind though it may be.

The emotional pain resulting from these kinds of injuries can continue for some time, even after the moral instinct is satisfied. The emotional pain is healed from within through empowerment and growth. When we can't stop hurting, it is not due to the effect of emotional pain alone. We continue to hurt ourselves by inflicting new pain upon old wounds.

What is this new pain?

Consider the father of the girl who was killed, for example. In his need to find compensation for the loss of his daughter, he crossed over the line that separates judgment from punishment. The court rightly judged the young man guilty, and the man admitted his guilt and was willing to accept some punishment. The father devised the terms of the punishment, which the court, probably inadvisably, accepted. In devising the punishment in such a way that the young man was forced to write out a check each week with the girl's name on it (on Friday, the day she was killed!), the father inflicted upon himself a weekly dose of new pain to feed an old wound.

Suppose you were to ask him, "Why don't you forgive the man and release yourself from this terrible tragedy? He has admitted his guilt. Nothing will bring your daughter back and you are tormenting yourself as well as punishing him."

His response might well be: "I owe it to my daughter to be sure that he pays for his carelessness. To forgive him and allow him to go free would be to cheapen her death, as though it meant nothing."

What the father is doing is what many of us do when we cannot let go of an old injury. Without being aware of it, we too "memorialize" our loss and, at regular intervals, review the transcript of the trial, and think of how sweet the punishment will be.

It is moral outrage which continues to demand punishment for the injuries which we have sustained. When these injuries can be recognized as being caused by someone else, we at least can bring the moral outrage to the bar of justice and demand a verdict, even if that verdict is rendered by someone whose moral authority lies outside of a court of law.

When the verdict does not result in internal satisfaction, we are forced to carry on the moral outrage through real or imagined punishment of others. In our example, the father heard the verdict of the court but was not able to internalize it in such a way as to meet the demands of his moral outrage. Thus he continually inflicts new pain upon the old wound under the guise of punishment for the offender.

Until a verdict satisfies our moral outrage, we are driven by the outrage to keep the hurt alive as our only witness to the crime. Punishment now becomes the bearer of our moral outrage. But punishment without a satisfying verdict is a crime against ourselves. To inflict punishment we continually retry the case. In this way, we present the evidence over and over again in order to justify the punishment.

When we can't stop hurting, it is because we have our private crime files, which are opened regularly so that we can review the gruesome evidence of our abuse at the hands of others. This always inflicts new pain upon our old wounds, but how else can a grievance be kept alive?

Forgiveness of an offender under these conditions would feel like a violation of the moral outrage. To be asked to "forgive and to forget" is to be asked to deny one's own sense of moral justice. The moral power of forgiveness cannot be exercised as long as moral outrage demands punishment. Forgiveness is not always possible.

When You Find It Difficult to Forgive

When we find it difficult to forgive, we should search for the unresolved moral outrage. The key to unlocking the power of forgiveness is the difference between a verdict which assigns guilt and punishment which is meted out to the one found guilty. Forgiveness has only to do with punishment, not the verdict of guilt or innocence. Let us see why.

Any injury to the self produces an instinctive moral judgment, usually in the form of an accusation against the one who caused the injury. Along with the moral judgment there is the desire to inflict punishment against the offender. A distinction between judgment and punishment is essential in order to understand the role of forgiveness in self-recovery. A judgment is something like the verdict rendered in a court of law. The offender is pronounced guilty or innocent. Punishment is the sentence imposed by the court. In determining punishment, extenuating circumstances may be taken into consideration so that not all who are judged guilty experience the same punishment.

Forgiveness does not absolve an offender from judgment, but releases the offender from punishment. For example, a good friend may betray you by sharing some information given in confidence with the result that you suffer shame and humiliation. The act of betrayal is a violation which produces an instinctive moral judgment against the one who committed the offense. If the friend, when confronted with the fact, acknowledges that betrayal indeed took place, then the issue of judgment has been resolved. Forgiveness is now possible because judgment has been rendered and the offense to the moral instinct of the self has been resolved. Releasing the offender from further punishment is what forgiveness does.

In the case of a victim of domestic violence or child abuse, there is a deep-seated moral offense which has been committed against the person abused. The victim needs to be supported and affirmed in making a judgment against the offense as well as against the offender that addresses the moral issue. Once this judgment has been rendered against the offender, the victim no longer is caught in self-blame. The feelings of outrage have now been dealt with, the feelings of anger can be allowed to be processed as emotion.

Outrage is grounded in a moral sense, while anger is primarily an emotion capable of change through new perceptions. Bringing forth a judgment against an offender draws outrage to a conclusion. The perception of the offender is now of one guilty of the offense. To continue to express condemnation once the judgment has been rendered is not necessary to satisfy the moral outrage. With the new perception of judgment rendered, the emotion of anger can be reduced and finally eliminated.

Judgment and punishment can sometimes become blurred in the feelings of the victim. Moral outrage and anger are not clearly distinguishable at an emotional level. Judgment and punishment are actually part of a two-step process. To judge another who has abused you as morally wrong is to satisfy the moral instinct of the self. To inflict punishment is a step beyond judgment. Punishing an offender for a wrong done is often beyond the power or competence of the victim.

When we have failed to render judgments fairly and accurately, we resort to punishment to compensate for the hurt we have suffered. Unfortunately, punishing others or ourselves never really satisfies the moral offense and never produces healing for the injured self. We cannot forgive ourselves or others until fair judgment has been reached. But we cannot do this without assistance and affirmation. Empowerment of the self must come from a source outside the self.

In the case of the father of the girl who was tragically killed, his moral outrage appears to have been fixed upon the punishment process. Thus he was unable to find the moral power of forgiveness. Until we discover the power of forgiveness, we can't stop hurting and we continue to hurt ourselves.

The Bible does not prohibit us from passing judgment against moral wrong. At the same time, it warns us about exacting vengeance against the offender. "Beloved, never avenge yourselves," writes the apostle Paul, "but leave room for the wrath of God; for it is written, 'Vengeance is mine, I will repay, says the Lord'" (Rom. 12:19; Deut. 32:35).

Once judgment has been rendered, the moral issue has been resolved and the basis for outrage removed. Anger, of course, continues, as do the feelings that the offender should suffer for the wrong done. Forgiveness does not excuse the wrongdoing nor bypass judgment. Forgiveness is only possible when the moral judgment has been rendered and supported. Forgiveness is itself a moral and spiritual achievement when it can be exercised. It is an acknowledgment that justice has been rendered through the moral judgment made and moves the self toward recovery by releasing the moral power of forgiveness.

Can We Forgive Where There is No Admission of Guilt?

Suppose the offender in the case of abuse denies the offense, as typically happens. When an offender does not acknowledge the wrong done through abuse, it is difficult, if not impossible, for forgiveness to be expressed. This is because forgiveness demands a moral threshold upon which to stand, ordinarily established when a judgment has been rendered.

James Leehan reminds us that it may be inappropriate to

expect forgiveness from the victim of abuse. The moral virtue of forgiveness offered to an offender requires an assignment of guilt as a moral context for forgiveness, which is not always present. In the case of child abuse, for example, victims of such trauma may be expected to express forgiveness as a moral or religious virtue.

> To expect forgiveness to be their initial response to abusive parents is to deny the reality of what was done to them. They need to deal with that reality in order to heal the scars which mar their lives. To berate them for their behavior may well convince them that they are not able to live up to the moral expectations or religious beliefs of any church or synagogue.[1]

Those who have been the victims of abusive behavior need an advocate to enter in and empower them to render a moral judgment against the offender, whether the offender acknowledges wrongdoing or not. This intervention serves to authenticate the outrage done to the self and serves to render a moral judgment against the offender on behalf of the victim. This does make forgiveness possible in the sense of giving over to God the punishment (vengeance) and freeing the self to be healed of the hurt and anger.

Behind all injuries to the self, regardless of the cause, there is a moral need for justice to be done. This can take the form of expressing a moral judgment on behalf of the injured person, even if the offender will not acknowledge responsibility.

In the case of Jeff, presented in the previous chapter, his father denied that he had sexually abused him, though it had been acknowledged by his mother. As I worked through the process of seeking a verdict with him, he began to see his father as really guilty of a crime. His feelings of having been violated were now affirmed as having moral validity. Reconciliation with his father would not be possible until his father accepted responsibility and offered repentance.

When we discussed what punishment should be brought against his father, Jeff began to have mixed feelings. "I have no desire to hurt my father," said Jeff. "I feel sorry for him. He must feel miserable inside knowing what he did but not being able to face it."

"Does this mean that you have no need or desire to punish him?" I asked.

He was quiet for a long time, but then said, "There is nothing to be gained by punishing him now. If forgiveness means that I still feel he is guilty but that I have no need or desire to punish him, then, yes, I can forgive him."

But what recourse do we have when the violation against us is the result of some malfunction of nature or simply bad luck? Where do we turn when life itself has dealt us a bad hand? How do we secure a verdict when there is no crime and we are only a victim of life's randomness?

Stop Hurting and Start Forgiving!

Susie has taught me a lesson that I can never forget. Afflicted with cerebral palsy since birth, she cannot dress or feed herself. She talks with difficulty and in words which emerge as twisted and tortured as the spastic motions required to force them out. With a passion for life that exceeds most others less restrained by physical limitations, she has completed college and a master's degree in theology, including several of my courses.

When she received her degree, I asked her what she intended to do, always seeing her within the boundaries which I had set for her. "Perhaps you will have a significant ministry to others who suffer handicaps in life," I suggested. "No," she said, "most of them haven't forgiven God for who they are, and I have."

Forgiving God for who I am! Indeed! Who should she hold responsible for the constricting limitations which imprison her free and joyous spirit within a body she cannot control? She expanded the horizon of her complaint, like Job of old, and laid the offense at the throne of God. When the Lord who created her did not dodge or duck, she concluded that the only freeing thing left was to forgive. Having lodged the charge against God with all of the emotional power at her disposal, she discovered that she also had the power to forgive Him.

Susie did not suppose that God had caused her birth deformity nor did she feel that He had willed this condition for some inscrutable purpose of His own. Her dealings with God were not theological but deeply existential. She sought to touch with her feelings the face of God and trace out there the profile of one who would take responsibility for her life without looking away. What she found encouraged her that in holding God responsible she found an ally in her predicament. Releasing God from blame became possible when God assumed responsibility. Her life now had two sides to it. The one side of her life was restricting and confining. The other side was open and freeing. This is what she meant by forgiving God for who she was. She let God become the other side to her life.

To free another person from an offense against one's own life is to free oneself, to discover a power which expands the horizons of self-awareness beyond all the given boundaries and burdens. Jesus gave us the key: "Whatever you loose on earth will be loosed in heaven" (Matt. 16:19). To discover the inner resources to forgive

God of an offense against one's life is to experience a spiritual power and freedom which stops the hurting and starts the healing. To forgive God is to stop punishing God with our anger and unbelief.

Not all of us have been abused and not many of us awakened in life to discover that we had a crippling or disfiguring birth defect. But all of us know what moral outrage is and what it is like to feel like a victim of unfairness, regardless of the source.

To discover that God is not the cause yet that He accepts responsibility is to be empowered to forgive, even God! In turning to God we can close the "crime file" we keep as evidence that we have been wounded and violated. With God as our friend, we have the moral authority to say that we have been vindicated, and that there is no longer need for punishment.

I hope that the tormented father has found the grace and power to forgive the destructive punishment meted out against the young man, and that both he and the man can receive their Fridays back again as a gift of life and not a monument to death. There is nothing so sweet as the taste of forgiveness and the absence of self-inflicted pain.

CHAPTER SEVEN

If Your Past Follows You, Give it a Present

It was the day before Christmas. John had called yesterday asking if we could get together for breakfast. A friend of many years, he and his wife had returned to spend Christmas in his home that had remained unsold for the past year, during which time he had relocated to the East Coast.

As we traded stories and brought our lives up to date, he suddenly said, "Ray, someday you need to write a book on The Ghosts of Christmas Past. On the way here, I drove by the house I lived in with my first wife, the church we attended, and the old neighborhood. The brokenness of those relationships hit me like a knife thrust in the side. Why is it that one's past continues to rise up and taunt you with your failures? Doesn't one ever get over these things?"

"John, do you know why your past follows you wherever you go? It is because it is *your* past. In the same way that your childhood always remains part of you, the events of your past are not appendages which can be cut off, but are woven into the fabric of your personal history."

"Thanks a lot!" he said with unconcealed sarcasm.

"What you're telling me is that my past is like a ball and chain. It will jerk me back into reality whenever I think that I have got something good going for me."

"You missed my point. I said that the past is *your* past. Because it is yours you can shape it and even change it by treating it as part of your present life and experience. If your past follows you, give it a present!"

"You have just earned your breakfast," he said. "Explain that and I'm buying."

The good news is that I did get a free meal. The bad news is that I spent more time talking than eating and never did finish my waffle! This is written for John, who bought me breakfast, and for you, the reader, who made your own investment in these words. I have a feeling we each have a need to come to terms with our own past.

The Past is Secured by Feelings, Not by Facts

Feelings, as I have said earlier in this book, are timeless. Events and actions occur in time; feelings are always present tense. I can think backwards to actions that I took or incidents that happened but I do not remember feelings like I do events and dates. If a memory stirs up feelings in me, these are not old feelings but present feelings.

Now it is true that remembrance of the past often causes the same feelings to rise up within me. For example, whenever I think about the time I made a miscalculation during navigator training for the Air Force and got hopelessly lost over the Gulf of Mexico, I have the same feeling of embarrassment and humiliation at having to call the pilot and ask him to use the radio to get us safely back to base. The incident occurred over 40 years ago, and is a matter of fact, as I am sure some document in the military files will verify, if my instructor faithfully recorded it.

What keeps this incident alive in my personal past, however, is my feelings, not the facts. I cannot recall the exact date, the name of the pilot, or anything else about the incident. It is the feeling that I have about myself that keeps the event from slipping out of my past, as a myriad of other incidents have.

The past is secured by feelings, not by facts. Feelings are always experienced in the present tense. What I think may be old feelings or emotional reactions which I experienced in the past but are really present feelings I have relating myself to previous actions and incidents. It is the memory of the incident that triggers the present feelings. Certain feelings became associated with the memory of the incident and thus give the appearance of being past feelings. In reality, there are no past feelings, only recollection of past events which stir up current feelings.

Feelings are always about the self, not about facts. The feelings which I had when I made a miscalculation and had to admit that I was lost were about being a failure. I had only myself to blame. Even worse, I was incapable of rectifying the mistake and felt an utter failure. These were negative feelings about myself. My self-esteem suffered a loss; I felt miserable and shamed. These are the feelings that fix this event in my personal past.

How do I know that I had these feelings at the time? Because recall of the incident stirs up some of the same feelings in me today. But I have other feelings about myself which are part of my present life. When my past follows me, I give it a present. I test out my feelings about being a failure because of a past incident by other feelings which I have about myself now—feelings which are positive and self-affirming.

As a result, the incident now becomes an anecdote, a story

that I tell. Secure in the feelings that I have about myself as a person of value despite many inadequacies and failures, I have revised my past by viewing it through the present.

It is true that we cannot rewrite history, but we can revise our own past. Because our past is secured by feelings, not by facts alone, we can revise our feelings about ourselves and thus about our past.

When I allow the memory of that incident to evoke feelings of utter failure, I find myself cramped into the narrow space of my navigator's cubicle, cut off from everyone else and alone with my feelings of self-blame. When I do this I allow the facts to take my feelings prisoner. My past then dominates my present.

But when I view the incident from the perspective of my present feelings about myself, the past is disarmed of its power to pull me back into that isolation chamber of failure and shame. When I have done that, I have revised my past by giving it a present.

Revising Our Past by Renewing the Present

"That's fine for you," John responded. "We have all had experiences similar to yours. But I have people in my past, not just miscalculations and failures. I have left behind a trail of broken promises and wounded people. Some of them have wounded me. My past is walking around in my present and I can't run away and hide."

"Fair enough," I replied. "Our past confronts us in the mailbox, in our address book, and in the tangled web of relationships we create but cannot entirely uncreate. You can divorce your wife but not so easily dispose of your children's mother."

"Yeah, now you're on the right track. These are some of the ghosts of my Christmases past. So what do I do?"

The key still lies with our feelings, I told John. The feelings which we have toward other people can change. And when they do, that usually marks the end of the relationship, or the beginning of abuse and even violence. The feelings which we have about ourselves, however, often do not change as easily.

For example, the breakdown of a marriage or of a long-term friendship, usually occurs through a series of incidents that lead to misunderstanding, mistrust, and feelings of hurt and sometimes guilt. We come away from such experiences with feelings about ourselves. If we feel violated, we will have the emotion of anger or revenge. If we have acted foolishly or wrongly and so destroyed the relationship, we may have feelings of guilt and shame.

When a relationship has ended it continues to be part of our past through the feelings which we continue to have toward ourselves with regard to the person or persons involved. Confronting the persons who are part of our past is really no different than recalling an incident in our past, except that we cannot practice avoidance by putting it out of our minds. In either case, whether our past follows us through memory or confronts us through persons, we can give our past a present by revising our feelings.

Let me use the well-known biblical story of King David as an example (2 Samuel 11-12). David, we are told, though married to the daughter of King Saul, lusted after the lovely Bathsheba, whom he saw bathing from the rooftop of the palace. Exercising his prerogative as King, he seduced her, and when it was discovered that she was pregnant, arranged to have her soldier husband killed and listed as a battle casualty. David then brought her to his house where she became one of his wives and the child was born in due season.

So far so good. David apparently succeeds in putting

the ugly affair behind him. It is his secret. Shortly, however-
er, Nathan the prophet, having received a revelation from
God, confronts David with the fact and elicits a confession.
While God would forgive his sin, Nathan assured him,
there would be consequences. The child would die.

There it is. A classic tale of betrayal, intrigue, guilt,
confession, and consequences. David now has his own
personal past. It will follow him wherever he goes. But
this is not the end.

When Solomon, David's next son was born to
Bathsheba, Nathan the Prophet again came to David with a
message from God, saying, "The Lord loved him."
Therefore, David gave another name to his son, Jedidiah,
which means "Beloved of the Lord" (2 Samuel 12:24-25).

The historian, in recounting this event, gives no clue as to
David's feelings. David himself was not so reticent. In two
Psalms, David describes the process by which he revised
his past through the creative expression of present feelings.

> While I kept silence, my body wasted away through
> my groaning all day long.
> For day and night your hand was heavy upon me; my
> strength was dried up as by the heat of summer.
> Then I acknowledged my sin to you, and I did not
> hide my iniquity; I said, "I will confess my transgres-
> sions to the Lord," and you forgave the guilt of my sin...
> Be glad in the Lord and rejoice, O righteous, and
> shout for joy, all you upright in heart.   Psalm 32

> Create in me a clean heart, O God, and put a new and
> right spirit within me.
> Do not cast me away from your presence, and do not
> take your holy spirit from me.
> Restore to me the joy of your salvation, and sustain
> in me a willing spirit.   Psalm 51

The use of the psalm in the case of David opens up to us an insight which must not elude us. Stories are reflective of the past and are mostly factual and not emotional. Psalms are expressions of strong emotions which embrace the facts but revise the feelings connected to the facts.

Each of us has a "historian self" and a self that composes psalms. It is the historian self which pulls us back into the past and recites the painful incidents so as to arouse the same negative feelings and emotions. When the historian dominates over the psalmist, the past tyrannizes and terrorizes the present.

The historian tells us that Nathan exposed David's secret and made public the desperate and tragic murder of Bathsheba's husband. David must now acknowledge the facts which are part of his past. The historian also tells us that Nathan brought a message of divine forgiveness and love to David, causing David to give a new name to his son, "Beloved of the Lord." The historian stands at a distance from this event, recording the actions but not having access to the attitudes and feelings.

The psalmist composes out of the present. The facts are put in perspective and described accurately as to their deadly effects. "While I kept silence, my body wasted away through my groaning all day long. For day and night your hand was heavy upon me; my strength was dried up as by the heat of summer." But the primary feelings expressed are those of joy and gladness. "Be glad in the Lord and rejoice, O righteous, and shout for joy, all you upright in heart." There is a refrain of healing and hope. "Restore to me the joy of your salvation, and sustain in me a willing spirit."

David has redirected his emotional energy. As long as his feelings were connected to the incidents and events in his past, he became spiritually and physically fatigued and oppressed. "While I kept silence, my body wasted away through my groaning all day long. For day and night your hand was heavy upon me; my strength was dried up as by the heat of summer." The discovery of his misdeed became material for the historian. The recovery from his past was the creative work of the psalmist.

We revise our past when we reinvest our feelings and emotional energy in the creative work of "restoring our soul" in the joy and presence of our God. The historian is the keeper of the archives of our past, the psalmist the creator of our future. We must liberate the psalmist in us and keep the historian in his place!

Reinvesting Our Emotional Energy

"John, your business is advising other people how to make wise and productive financial investments. But your own emotional portfolio is depleting your life through investment of emotional energy in nonproductive stock issues out of the past. The emotional energy you are expending in maintaining your ghosts, as you put it, is robbing you of the creative power to expand the horizons of your present and future."

"I hear you," he replied. "But where do I find the resources to invest myself in a new venture when I am paying off all of these old debts? To follow up on your metaphor of investment counseling, where do I find the venture capital in my emotional and spiritual life to risk on the future? My track record is not all that good!"

"You have made a start, " I said. "You have discovered that your past is being maintained by your feelings. I am no Nathan the Prophet, but I can tell you that God can stir up feelings in you that are richer and deeper than guilt, shame or despair. You use a computer don't you? The software programs provide menus that open up and make accessible the vast power of the computer. Let me provide a sample of a menu that you can use to work on your own recovery."

1. Conduct an emotional audit.

An emotional audit is taken by identifying and listing the negative feelings which are stirred up in us by incidents, events or persons from our past on a recurring basis. The feelings can be identified on a scale of intensity, as well as frequency. Emotions, such as anger, grief, hurt, fear, shame and guilt are strongly negative feelings which rate high on the intensity scale. Emotions such as sadness, regret, sorrow, tend to be less intense though of longer duration.

When incidents in our past trigger negative feelings of high intensity which reoccur frequently, the emotional drain can be severe and chronic. Lower intensity emotions related to past events may not be identified as clearly related to any specific event or incident, but may have a cumulative effect, resulting in a depletion of emotional strength.

One form of depression might be the result of an overload of such negative feelings. The emotional system shuts down in an effort to block the continued depletion of emotional energy. In some cases, depression may actually be viewed as a warning system alerting us to the need for an emotional audit of the kind I am suggesting.

The purpose of such an audit is to shift the focus from the past incident or event to the feeling we are encountering. Our past follows us through these feelings, whether by memory or through contact with persons and places which we encounter in our daily lives. The feelings generated by these incidents are located in our present state, however, and are thus subject to revision and redistribution.

For example, John expressed strong feelings of guilt over the failure of his first marriage, which he blamed on his own preoccupation with business and neglect of marital relations. Following his divorce, he became involved with a woman for a number of years and a new network of related persons. When that relationship ended, he entered another which eventually led to marriage. The children from the first marriage and the house in which he lived with his former girlfriend all continue to demand maintenance. He thus has a constellation of places, events, and relationships, each of which connects him with the feelings of guilt and failure of his first marriage.

When he conducts his emotional audit, he will discover how often he encounters his past and how frequently the intense emotion of guilt occurs in his present life. If the emotional energy he is expending on the maintenance of his past life is greater than he has available to spend on his current marriage, he knows that he is in trouble.

He thinks that these "ghosts" of the past carry old emotional pain which continues to haunt and torment him. As a consequence, he considers these feelings "old debts" which he must pay, as though in suffering the pain he can finally atone for the guilt and put his past behind him.

But this is entirely wrong. Current emotional pain is never the necessary consequence of past failure or personal injury. Feelings are not consequences; they are not penalties which we must bear for past actions. Consequences, like the actions that cause them, are things about which we have feelings. They are part of the facts. But consequences are never themselves the feelings. Feelings, as I have said, are about ourselves, not about the facts or the events.

When we have conducted an emotional audit, we have

identified the psychic wounds through which our feelings are bleeding unstaunched. This is the first step in recovery from the revenge of the past.

2. Confess the presence of unconditional love.

The association of confession with wrongdoing is one of the oldest traditions of the Judeo-Christian tradition. David follows his emotional audit with a personal acknowledgment of sin: "Then I acknowledged my sin to you, and I did not hide my iniquity; I said, 'I will confess my transgressions to the Lord,' and you forgave the guilt of my sin" (Psalm 32:5).

From the historical record of David's actions, however, we discovered that he only acknowledged his wrongdoing when confronted by Nathan the Prophet. It was also Nathan who gave him assurance of forgiveness. "Now the Lord has put away your sin; you shall not die" (2 Samuel 12:13).

There were indeed consequences of his actions; the child born to Bathsheba died. Confession is not a way of avoiding consequences, but of "restoring our souls," to use a somewhat quaint, but comforting biblical expression. "Do not take your Holy Spirit from me," was David's prayer. "Restore to me the joy of your salvation, and sustain in me a willing spirit" (Psalm 51:12).

Nathan was a person who evidently had the unusual quality of empowering another person in the moment of their greatest vulnerability and weakness. This is what is meant by unconditional love. It is a love which permits no deception but which offers healing and hope with no strings attached.

Dietrich Bonhoeffer, a German pastor who entered into a conspiracy against Hitler for the sake of the Jews who were being systematically tortured and exterminated, spoke often of the reality of human relationships as a context and criterion for the reality of divine love and forgiveness. Aware of the futility many people experience in attempting to find healing and restoration in their private appeals to God for forgiveness, he suggested that it is only in the context of the other person that we really find acceptance and healing.

> In confession a man breaks through to certainty. Why is it that it is often easier for us to confess our sins to God than to a brother? God is holy and sinless, He is a just judge of evil and the enemy of all disobedience. But a brother is sinful as we are. He knows from his own experience the dark night of secret sin. Why should we not find it easier to go to a brother than to the holy God? But if we do, we must ask ourselves whether we have not often been deceiving ourselves with our confession of sin to God, whether we have not rather been confessing our sins to ourselves and also granting ourselves absolution. . . . Our brother breaks the circle of self-deception. A man who confesses his sins in the presence of a brother knows that he is no longer alone with himself; he experiences the presence of God in the reality of the other person. . . . Mutual, brotherly confession is given to us by God in order that we may be sure of divine forgiveness.[1]

It is not only our own act of wrongdoing which destroys self-acceptance and self-love. When others violate our personal dignity and integrity, we are also deprived of the health and wholeness which is necessary to our own well-being. In other words, the sins of others who act against us can damage our souls as much as do our own sins.

Confession has to do with restoration, not regret. Confession has to do with renewal not with ritualistic self-abuse. Confession is moving out of isolation into relationship, out of pain into pleasure.

Confession has to do with inner healing and the restoration of self-acceptance and self-love. Self-love is not a feeling that we can achieve on our own. Rather, it is the reflection within our own self of the unconditional love of others.

Confession is good for the soul, we are told. That is true, but it can become a trite saying and cheap grace. What is good for the soul is the restoration and healing of our wounded spirits. Confession in the context of unconditional love is not a religious ritual but a human and personal encounter which bares our soul in pain and bathes it with the healing water of acceptance and affirmation.

In confession we break through to certainty, Bonhoeffer reminds us. Certainty delivers us from the anxious feelings that we have yet to be punished enough for our past. Certainty frees us from the compulsive need to manipulate others into giving us assurances to feed our deeply entrenched insecurities. In reaching certainty, we have cut the infinite distance between us and divine love down to an arm's length.

Whatever else one might think of Jesus of Nazareth, those who came to know Him best discovered the certainty that can only come from the soul that has been touched by the heart of God. "I am the way, and the truth, and the life," Jesus told His disciples. "Whoever has seen me has seen the Father" (John 14:6, 9). But this was said *after* Jesus had washed their feet and wiped them with a towel (John 13:1-11)!

"John, you are on the verge of breaking through to this certainty," I said. "Nothing less than the Spirit of God can restore your own spirit. And this will come when you are most vulnerable, but also when you are most protected and affirmed by those who are there for you with unconditional love. You will recognize them when, in a manner of speaking, they take your feet in their hands."

3. Consecrate a new birth of hope.

Do you remember the incident concerning the second son born to David by Bathsheba? David gave him the name Solomon. Nathan the Prophet brought a message from God, indicating that this child was "beloved of the Lord." Therefore David gave him an additional name, Jedidiah, which literally embodied that promise.

We cannot shift our feelings through an act of our own will. Even though we have discovered through an emotional audit that we are expending our emotional energy on events which take much but give back nothing, we remain powerless. As John complained, "Where do I find the resources to invest myself in a new venture when I am paying off all of these old debts?"

For David, the intervention was of divine origin, as I suspect all creative beginnings are. Having the consequence of his actions explained to him by the prophet, and accepting those consequences as facts, David no longer felt it necessary to continue his negative feelings about himself as consequences. But where should he now invest his feelings?

Again, the prophet brought a divine word. The child is "loved by the Lord." This gave David a new birth of hope, which he consecrated by blessing the child and giving it a name signifying this new beginning.

In our emotional dilemmas, we make hundreds of new beginnings and a thousand promises to ourselves, as well as to others. But these all are swept away by the undertow of our negative emotions flowing back out to the empty sea of our past.

We can only consecrate what has already been hallowed, as Abraham Lincoln saw with almost divine perception, when he gave his memorable address on the battlefield at Gettysburg, where so many thousands gave their lives in the hopeless war between the states. The ground where brave men gave their lives became hallowed by their sacrifice. So too the Wall of Remembrance in Washington, D.C. hallows the lives of those who gave their lives in the tragic war in Viet Nam. These are names which rise up out of the past to stir the emotions of gratitude and honor.

But God hallows life, not death, through the bringing of divine love as a benediction upon the heads of our own offspring, conceived in folly and foolishness, though they be.

Somewhere, in the life of each one of us, there is something which God loves and blesses. Disguised as a friend, counselor, or sometimes even a priest, a Nathan speaks the word of God concerning that which God loves in us. This stirs and attracts our feelings in a far deeper and richer way than the events and incidents in our past. This is what David discovered, and this is what led him to consecrate the gift of forgiveness and hope.

4. Compose a psalm of deliverance and celebration.

The historian in each of has been carefully trained by parents and teachers to take note of discrepancies and to mark the red-letter days in our lives. Unfortunately the former occur with greater frequency than the latter! Our past is preserved, if you can picture it, by an efficient but faceless librarian who has never misfiled or lost a date or document that causes us pain, but who disappears into the stacks when we are on a search for the elusive fragment of personal esteem! How could we have trained one with such devilish efficiency and such poor manners!

The psalmist in us receives little recognition and less reward. David, I assume, did not become a psalmist as preparation for becoming a King. It was in his early life as a shepherd that he sang his feelings into song. Sheep are a passive but also permissive audience. Shepherding is a lonely but exquisitely lovely commune with the self. Kahlil Gibran once wrote, a great singer is someone who "sings our silences."[2] I would add, "A psalmist is one who uses words to make feelings visible."

Our journey of self-recovery has not begun until we have written our psalm—and published it! The Scriptures of the Hebrew people not only contained a book of Chronicles but a book of Psalms! They kept the historian to remind them of their origin and pilgrimage with God. But they sang the Psalms to consecrate their lives with feelings of gratitude and praise to God.

The breakthrough to certainty for David did not occur only through confession but also through the communication of his feelings. The composing of our psalm is for the purpose of bringing the psalmist in us, like Cinderella, out of the kitchen into the living area to sit, with our treasured and trusted friends, at the head of the table. This place, ordinarily reserved for the historian self, will feel uncomfortable and uneasy for the psalmist self. This is due to our neglect, not the intrinsic inadequacy of the psalmist!

As an exercise, one should read a Psalm of David each day for a month before attempting to write one's own psalm. One needs to become familiar with the art of using past events as a framework for painting word pictures with feeling. Remember, the psalm should contain some elements of the emotional audit, the confession in the context of unconditional love, and the consecration of a new birth of hope.

The psalm is published when it is shared with a trusted person, like Nathan the Prophet, to do as he or she pleases with it! It cannot be taken back, nor protected by any "right of privacy." Do it!

CHAPTER EIGHT

If Misfortune Strikes, Strike Back

Divide your means seven ways, or even eight, for you do
not know what disaster may happen on earth.

In the morning sow your seed, and at evening do not let
your hands be idle; for you do not know which will
prosper, this or that, or whether both alike will be
good (Ecclesiastes 11:2, 6).

It was Saturday evening and harvest time. I was but a
young boy, and had to stretch my legs to match my father's
stride as we walked out into the barley field. The ripening
grain flowed almost to my father's waist, and to my shoul-
ders, as we waded into this river of gold.

"It's about ready," my father said, as much to himself as
to me. "Come Monday we will begin cutting."

I don't know what his dreams were that night, but mine
were of the excitement of following the horsedrawn harvester around the field, watching the bundles spew out,
each tied with rough twine by the clicking fingers of the
mechanical apparatus. My job was to stack them into

shocks with the grain ends on top, forming a bearded bouquet of sunlit straw.

But it was not to be. On Sunday afternoon, a thunderstorm marched across the prairie stabbing the ground with lightening strokes and pelting all that lay within its glowering stride with pounding hailstones. The frozen pellets of ice drove animals under cover, tore shingles off the roof, and cut the standing grain to a mangled mass of broken straw.

When the storm had passed, we walked once more out into the field. He surveyed the sodden field with eyes as practiced in measuring chaos as they were in envisioning a harvest. When he spoke, it was directly to me, as though he were depositing the words, like seeds, into a freshly plowed field.

"Son," he said, "when this field dries out we will begin to work it to keep the weeds down. A fall rain is good for the subsoil. We still have seed for planting in the spring, and it will grow a better crop next year for all of this."

This was surely not his first crop loss, nor would it be his last. I have attempted to reflect on those years to assess his feelings which, if they were expressed, were beyond my capacity to perceive at the time. This I know. There was no cursing of the earth and no angry gestures toward Heaven. There was no apparent self-recrimination for failing to have begun the harvest earlier.

Misfortune had struck. And he struck back in the only way that he knew how. He wagered the power of the seed against the fury of the storm. By the time he had returned to the farmhouse that Sunday evening, he had decided which crop he would plant in that field! He had only lost a harvest, not his hope.

Psychologists might have considered this lack of emotional outrage unhealthy. Better to express anger at the cruel tricks of nature than to repress and internalize the feelings of grief and disappointment. My father, they would assure me, was a typical inexpressive male. I doubt it! No other person has communicated such a depth of feeling and a capacity for faith as he expressed in my presence.

We can only have strong feelings for that which has the capacity to break our hearts. We can only mend a broken heart by sowing the seeds for a future harvest. He loved the soil and the seed more than the harvest! There is a lesson to be learned here.

This I discovered from living so dependent upon the cycle of nature, with life lived between the sowing and the reaping. Life is meant to be lived from one sowing to another, not one harvest to another. The good harvest is a time of rejoicing and thanksgiving at life's bountifulness. But those who live by the harvest, die by the harvest.

In my youth I was more fascinated and taken up with harvest time than planting time. The drudgery of chores in the winter and the bleak days of early spring planting seldom stirred my soul. The care of the crops during the hot days of summer was a battle against weeds, insects, and the worrisome weather. I had no positive feelings for these days and duties. My emotions were fixed on harvest time!

Diversifying Your Emotional Investments

Emotions need to mature in much the same ways as our body and mind. Immature emotions seem untamed and lacking in discipline, because they are stirred by dreams more than by duty, moved by success more than by sacrifice. To extend the metaphor of sowing and reaping, when emotions are attached to the promise of the harvest more than to the power of the seed, they can be fragile and fearful. The emotion of hope for a bountiful harvest is closely attended by a fear that it will be stolen from us at the last minute. We have attached the emotions of childhood to many dreams which have shattered and to many wishes which remain unfulfilled.

The emotions which become fixed on the harvest alone are unreliable and unstable. When we invest all of our emotional energy in attaining goals that are subject to random misfortunes that can strike without warning, we are like children who lunge from one emotional crisis to another. It is not that emotion itself is unreliable and a source of instability. What causes emotional chaos in our lives is not emotion itself but the collapse into chaos of that upon which we have fastened our feelings. When misfortune strikes, the child is devastated and left without mooring amidst the flood of feelings.

Paul, the apostle, took the measure of his own growth toward maturity and offered wise counsel to others when he wrote: "When I was a child, I spoke like a child, I thought like a child, I reasoned like a child; when I became an adult, I put an end to childish ways" (1 Cor. 13:11).

A "childish" way of living risks personal fulfillment on the attaining of one object or experience as the only thing that will bring satisfaction. Children have not learned to diversify their emotional investment in life.

The teacher of wisdom in ancient Israel wrote: "Divide your means seven ways, or even eight, for you do not know what disaster may happen on earth" (Ecclesiastes 11:2). Life teaches one not to "put all of our eggs in one basket." There is emotional wisdom in this as well. The dividing up of our emotional investments leaves us with resources to strike back when misfortune strikes.

In my youth and inexperience, I saw the barley harvest as the only thing that counted. I had no comprehension of the fact that, for my father, this was a misfortune that would cause some hardship and personal disappointment, but that it was not the collapse of his life investment in farming. Not only had he learned to diversify his crops so that the harvest season was spread out over a longer period, he had learned to diversify his emotional investment in life. No misfortune at harvest time had the power to rob him of the self-fulfillment experienced at planting time!

He struck back in the face of the misfortune by launching another season of preparing and planning. There is emotional wisdom and personal power in taking the initiative in the face of life's misfortunes. Life teaches us that emotional maturity results from emotional diversity. Not every seed will produce a harvest, but the planting of seeds exercises a step of faith and the renewal of hope.

As we experience life in moving out of our youth into adulthood, we begin to experience the losses and failures that come with every venture. The word "misfortune" captures exactly the emotional impact of a sudden loss. One definition of fortune is "prosperity attained partly through luck." To have a beneficial growing season and good weather through harvest is fortunate for the farmer. Despite the wisdom, skill and hard labor that goes into the growing of a crop, the harvest is largely dependent upon good fortune. To lose the harvest, in the end, is unfortunate.

Life is a venture where good fortune is desired and misfortune is feared. If we wish to pay the premium, we can insure against some of life's misfortunes which have a material or financial impact. Insurance, however, does not prevent misfortune, it only serves to compensate for the loss caused by misfortune.

When we wager our life in relationships and undertake commitments where we stand to lose what we love the most, misfortune is a loss against which there is no insurance or means for compensation. Grief over a loss of that which we have loved and in which we have made investments of passion and patience, is heartbreaking. We have our deepest feelings for that which has the capacity to break our hearts. At the same time, we must make emotional investments in order to plant the seed of love in the soil of life. The risk of failure is no reason not to go forth and plant.

An emotional venture as well as a financial investment may be a life-long dream or even a measure of one's own worth. When misfortune strikes, it can break our heart as well as our bank account. There is no insurance against an emotional bankruptcy.

Marriage vows are exchanged with an extravagant outpouring of promise and prosperity. Uncertainties are suppressed and good fortune grasped as a harvest of happiness. But there has been little sowing and less preparation of the soil. In some cases, the harvest is lost before the planting is begun. Our intentions are realistic and honest. Disaster is woven along with delight into the very words of the marriage vow: in plenty and in want, in joy and in sorrow, in sickness and in health. Misfortune is the invisible attendant at the wedding celebration.

Receiving children as a gift of life, either through natural birth or adoption, begins the cycle of sowing and reaping. Small misfortunes are the training track for the long distance run. Where once the emotions were stirred by a prize to be gained, they are now demanded as a price to be paid. Life mingles with life.

The Miami University poet, Ridgely Torrence, captures the almost imperceptible joining of life with loss in a few crisp words.

THE SON

I heard an old farm-wife,
   Selling some barley,
Mingle her life with life
   And the name "Charley."

Saying, "The crop's all in
   We're about through now;
Long nights will soon begin,
   We're just us two now.

"Twelve bushel at sixty cents,
   It's all I carried—
He sickened making fence;
   He was to be married—

"It feels like frost was near—
   His hair was curly,
The Spring was late that year,
   But the harvest early."[1]

The Secret of a Grace-Empowered Life

There are some who seem to absorb misfortune into the pace of life without missing a step. They may stumble but not fall. They experience defeat but do not retreat. Their lives are not marked by an unusual amount of luck; still, they demonstrate an extraordinary measure of pluck. What is the secret of their capacity to sustain faith and hope, sometimes against great odds? Are they saints endowed with some special gift of the gods, or are they ordinary people, like all of us, empowered by grace? The latter, I believe.

We are each created a special self, not just manufactured from a mold. The love and grace of God, our Creator, are seeds to be sown in the soil of the self.

Love is not like the sunshine which warms the soil, but like the seed which responds to the care of the self.

Grace is not like the rain which waters the earth, but the life of the seed which is sown in love for the self.

Hope dies when care for the self is neglected. Love cannot grow when there is not faith for it to be sown in the soil of the self. Faith grows strong when self-care receives the gifts of God's love and grace.

Let me suggest some ways in which we, as ordinary people, can live an extraordinary life empowered by the grace of God.

Exercise the gift of faith

The gift of faith is the power of God's grace which empowers the self to truly desire what is promised by God in fulfillment of a personal life venture. The child does not venture into the future, but grasps life in the present. The child does not yet have goals which lie beyond what can be gained in the moment. Faith is what connects the hunger of the self to the hope of the self that fulfillment is within one's reach. Without the hunger, there is no fuel to fire up faith. Without the hope, there is no mark on which faith can set its sight.

I am now convinced that faith is exercised when we attach this hunger for self-fulfillment to a task within our reach but which promises a result not within our power to fulfill. Faith does not create its own value over and against the value of the self. Rather, faith transforms the value of self-fulfillment from its "childish" grasp on what is immediately at hand to the abiding value of what is promised and for which one hopes.

This is why the author of Hebrews could write, "Faith is the assurance of things hoped for, the conviction of things not seen" (Hebrews 11:1). The writer goes on to say that faith brought benefits and rewards to those who possessed it. By faith, the ancestors "received approval." By faith Abel's sacrifice was "more acceptable," and he "received approval." By faith Abraham "received an inheritance." In exercising faith, these people received immediate value for the lives which they lived while gaining assurance of that for which they hoped.

Faith is rooted in the hunger of the self for recognition, for approval, and those values for which the greatest sacrifice is not too much. We learn to have faith when we discover this hunger and dare to hope for fulfillment.

We exercise the gift of faith by visualizing the planting of new seeds amidst the disaster of a ruined harvest. My father looked out over the field where his hopes for a harvest lay in ruins and envisioned first, a new planting season, with hope for a better harvest. Faith turns to the task of planting. Hope is given new life with the sowing of seed in expectation of a new harvest.

Those who live by the harvest, die by the harvest. When our emotions are invested only in the hope for a harvest without faith in the power of the seed, we lose sight of our participation in the cycle of renewal which unlocks the storehouse of the grace of God.

When we envision the planting of new seeds, we have looked past the ruins of a failed harvest of hope toward the coming spring with its time of growth and renewal. Preparing for a harvest takes only a few days, or even hours. Preparing to sow new seeds requires months of waiting through the long winter, anticipating the warm spring sun and the stirring of the soil. Sowing has to do with preparing the seed, preparing the soil, and attending the new growth.

No better metaphor for the exercising of faith can be found than that of sowing, for it requires an investment of the self in that which lies within our power to perform but not within our power to produce.

Those who demonstrate the unusual power to strike back when misfortune strikes are those who have learned to exercise the power of faith. They save some seed from every harvest and sow it in the fields savaged by the cruel storms of life. These people are not exceptional saints, they are ordinary sowers empowered by grace.

Practice the art of self-care

One of the most memorable and misunderstood teachings of Jesus must be his exhortation, "do not worry [take no care] for your life" (Matt. 6:25). This has often been interpreted as though Jesus were warning us against self-care. On the contrary, he was warning against attempting to secure our lives by dependence upon things which lay outside our control.

The lilies of the field, and the birds of the air, Jesus reminds us, do not attempt to control their lives, but simply live their lives as given by their Creator. Self-care is quite different from self-preservation. Self-preservation attempts to control our fortune in life. Self-care is the insurance of the value of life despite misfortune.

When Jesus says, "Truly I tell you, unless you change and become like children, you will never enter the kingdom of Heaven" (Matt. 18:3), He implies that there is some essential goodness which the child possesses and which needs to be cared for. This childlike joy and happiness may be the motivating source for self-fulfillment that is indispensable to faith, hope, and love. The self-love which is typical of the child is the basis for self-care in the adult.

When Jesus exhorts us to "receive the kingdom of God as a little child," it means that we rediscover the longing which opens us up to God's love and the fulfillment of the self in another. It may well be that Jesus was reminding adults that they carry within them a childlike longing which can become a childish bent toward controlling their own destiny and securing their own gratification through controlling their own fortune.

Practicing the art of self-care begins with the maintenance of our lives, including the health and productivity of that which is given to us to be and do.

As I look back upon the remarkable capacity of my father to strike back at the misfortune of a ruined harvest by envisioning a new planting season on that very field, I think that I can discern the secret of self-care. He maintained a sense of self-identity and self-worth through the diligence and faithfulness with which he fulfilled his vocation in life. His life was that of one who cared for the soil, the seed, and his livestock.

He practiced self-care by finding self-worth in his role as a planter, not merely a harvester. He cared for himself by caring for that which was an extension of his life. The fortunes of the harvest lay outside his control. A ruined harvest was a loss to be felt and to be grieved. But it was not a judgment against himself. The crops may fail, but not the one who cares for them.

In the technical jargon of agricultural science, a farmer is one who practices the art of "husbandry," defined in the dictionary as "one that plows and cultivates land." My own college degree is in agriculture with a major in "animal husbandry." The art of "husbandry" is that of caring for that which comprises one's livelihood.

The word "husband," therefore, represents a care for life as well as a role in life, particularly in marriage. The apostle Paul counsels husbands to "love their wives as they do their own bodies. . . . For no one ever hates his own body, but he nourishes and tenderly cares for it . . ." (Ephesians 5:28, 29).

Paul's point is that the care of a husband for his wife is to be of the same quality as the self-care which the man expresses towards his own life. Self-care is the source of the care which one expresses towards others and life itself.

The practice of the art of self-care begins with the caring for that which contributes to our sense of integrity, dignity, and self-worth. Refusing to blame oneself or others for misfortune begins by not counting toward one's own credit that which is merely good fortune. The extended metaphor of sowing seed has much to do with self-care within our home environments. The task of investing our emotions again and again after disaster strikes is one that confronts us all.

The prudent farmer preserves and cares for the seed to be sown for a future harvest. Self-care is prudent care for oneself and the exercising of faith by investing love in prepared soil for the sake of a better harvest.

Lay up some treasure for yourself

In an informal sermon I once read the text of Scripture from Matthew's version of the Sermon on the Mount: "Do not store up for yourselves treasures on earth, . . . but store up for God treasures in heaven." I paused for several seconds to see what effect this rendering of Matthew's text might have upon my listeners. Suddenly a woman sitting in the front row with her Bible open exclaimed, "That is not what my Bible says!" I asked her to read what her

Bible said and she read, "lay up for *yourselves* treasures in heaven."

I pretended to be amazed and asked if anyone else had a Bible with that reading. When others began to look at the text for themselves, they all agreed, Jesus said to "lay up for *ourselves* treasures in heaven," not "for God!" What was disturbing was that in substituting "for God" rather than "for yourselves" in reading the text, only one person heard that as wrong. We have all become so accustomed to the teaching that nothing should be done "for ourselves" that it sounded quite right that we should lay up treasure in Heaven for God, not for ourselves!

Every so often, we need to draw up a statement of our personal net worth. This is often done when we apply for credit, by subtracting our financial liabilities from our assets. When our liabilities exceed our assets, then we are in financial trouble! A financial consultant can often provide help in suggesting better methods of money management, debt consolidation, and better discipline in the use of credit purchases.

In somewhat the same way, we can conduct an inventory of our investments in that which accumulates "treasure" *for us* in heaven. When we are investing more of our lives in others here on earth and God who is in Heaven, than we are accumulating for ourselves, we are not practicing good self-care. I am not sure as to what a treasure in Heaven might be, but I know very well what it means when something is preserved *for myself*! Heaven is the promise of a harvest which no misfortune here on earth can ruin.

My father's net worth was not very much from a financial standpoint. The ruined barley harvest was but one of many misfortunes which struck during his lifetime. But his personal net worth grew steadily as he exercised faith, practiced good self-care, and accumulated treasure for himself in Heaven. He never sought revenge against misfortune. But he struck back through the investment of his life in a ritual of preparing the soil and planting the seed. I think that he knew what I am talking about, though he never spoke of it. I speak of it, for him and for myself. It is the gift of a Grace-empowered life, and God is the giver.

> The Lord has done great things for us, and we rejoiced.
>   Restore our fortunes, O lord, like the watercourses in
>   the Negeb.
> May those who sow in tears reap with shouts of joy.
> Those who go out weeping, bearing the seed for sowing,
>   shall come home with shouts of joy, carrying their
>   sheave   (Psalm 126).

PART THREE

SELF-RECOVERY

The Journey to Freedom

CHAPTER NINE

Recovering from Unhealed Childhood Trauma

How far back into your early childhood can you push your memory? Try as I might, I have no conscious memory of any experience or event prior to the age of five. I have been told that I lived with my parents and older brother on one farm for the first four years of my life, and then moved to a different one about the time I was five.

What seems astounding to me, is that not a single memory survives of those five years! My memory bank simply will not produce any feeling or experience during those years. I wonder if that is not true for most of us?

I peer at the black and white pictures, now yellowing with age, taken by my parents during those early years, and gaze with curiosity and wonder at the child I see that bears my name. Even these pictures stir no memory. All of those delicious, terrifying, comforting and exciting tastes, sounds, smells and touches lie buried in some inaccessible vault for which I have no combination. I remember the smell of tobacco smoke in my father's clothes, and the comforting feel of his work-worn hands as a boy of six, but not of his tender touch and soft voice when he played with me as a toddler learning to walk. Is it a blessing or a tragedy that we do not remember the experiences of our early childhood?

Experience of family is necessary for our development as persons, but not all experience of family is positive, as Theodore Roszak reminds us.

> The violation of personhood begins in the cradle, if not in the womb. . . . We are born into other people's intentions. We learn our names and our natures at their hands, and they cannot teach us more truth than they know or will freely tell. Can there be families whose love is not treason against our natural vocation? . . . We know that every ideal that supports the family has been used to tell a lie.[1]

Even though our intentions are good, we are not perfect parents. And with our imperfect love also comes violations of those that we love. In some cases, it is well that we do not remember the wrongs committed. And if the price we pay is to sacrifice the remembrance of the tokens of love, then perhaps that is a bargain we make with ourselves. But there is also a price to pay for not remembering and not feeling, as we shall see.

As I write this, we have just had two of our grandsons, ages two and three, in our house for a week. Those were days filled with shared experiences which appeared to touch their lives as deeply and profoundly as ours. How can it be, I ask myself, that when they grow older they will have no conscious memory of something so significant and formative in their lives? I desire for them the memory of that which I see them experience, for part of me is carried deep within those feelings and experiences.

I realize, of course, that feelings are timeless and are not preserved by conscious memory in chronological order. I also realize that some of the most powerful forces that impact our lives as adults are the result of childhood experiences which have been lost to conscious memory or repressed by that same power of consciousness.

The Relation of Memory to Feeling

Memory is a fascinating function of the life of the self. To lose one's memory is a terrible thing. To look intently into the eyes of a parent suffering from Alzheimer's disease, and have that person stare back with no recognition is a shock to our senses and a loss for which we hardly know how to grieve. We gently chide ourselves for becoming forgetful, but are impatient and concerned for others whose memory seems to be slipping.

There are at least two levels of memory. At the conscious level, memory is primarily a function of the mind and as such, is one aspect of what we call rationality, or reason. Loss of memory at the conscious level does not destroy one's rational process, but it distorts the relation of the self to others and to one's personal history. These distortions give the appearance of irrationality.

At the subconscious level, there is another memory tape that apparently records data which are not always accessible to our conscious mind. Witnesses of a crime, or of an automobile accident, for example, may not be able to recall vital information such as a license plate number, or distinctive features of a person's appearance or dress. Under hypnosis, the mind can often retrieve such information which was recorded at the subconscious level during one's experience of the event.

It is still true, however, that both subconscious and conscious memory is basically a function of the mind, depending upon some level of brain cell activity. Feelings, whether positive or negative, are not directly imbedded in memory. This is why we can have feelings with no memory attached, and memory of events but with no feelings experienced.

The core of the self is feeling, not thought. Memory has to do with the relation of the self to its existence in time and space. Memory is the relation of the self to objects, such as numbers, persons, events. Feeling is the relation of the self to itself. Thought can arouse feeling, but feeling cannot always awaken thought.

When Ann came to me for pastoral counseling she was distraught over her inability to control her feelings toward her mother. These feelings were so negative and powerful that her marriage was in difficulty and her relationship with her children was becoming bitter and spiteful.

As she told her story, it became clear that she had never seen her mother and had no memory of her. What she had discovered only six months previously, was that her mother had abandoned her when she was but one year old, and left her to be raised by her father. She had been told by her father and had believed all of her life that her mother died when she was born. Now, as it turns out, this was not true. The fact is that her mother did abandon her, even though Ann had no conscious memory of that fact. Her father felt that it would now be better for her to know the truth.

This new knowledge aroused feelings of anger, outrage and resentment at her mother, whom she could not remember. As Ann continued to think about it, her feelings against her mother became so strong that she became obsessed with them to the point where she was unable to function in a normal and healthy way with other important people in her life.

But what of that one-year-old child? What feelings

would that little girl have had at the sudden disappearance of her mother from her life? Are the feelings that Ann now has a resurgence of those unexpressed feelings or are they the result of the thoughts which she now has about the abandonment? In all likelihood both.

Recovery from Normal Childhood Trauma

Only children know the feelings of being a child, and they cannot tell us what they know, for their feelings as yet have no thoughts. Attaching thoughts to feelings is a process to be learned, a skill to be acquired. Some of us are slow learners, and others have learning disabilities at the level of communicating feelings. Lack of effective communication skills in interpersonal relationships can be traced to the detachment of feeling from thought.

Children can be observed, however, in how they handle their feelings. In a healthy context of supportive love and care, children feel safe, secure, and valued when held, recognized, affirmed, and heard. Children seek attention because they hunger for the good feelings which result. When these good feelings are reinforced, day by day and by the same people, a core of self-worth and positive self-esteem is being developed.

These same children will also experience pain, frustration and anger at regular intervals as they cope with living in a world that is not user-friendly. They will experience bumps and bruises which cause physical pain. Their toys will be taken by other children and their need for instant self-gratification delayed through parental discretion and discipline. These are some of the normal childhood traumas we all have experienced.

When children experience a healthy relationship of supportive love and care, adults marvel at how quickly the strong negative feelings generated by frustration of their need for pleasure seem to disappear. When children have a strong sense of security and feel loved and cared for, they recover quickly from what appear to be traumatic incidents of hurt bodies and hurt feelings.

The recovery process for children who have a strong sense of positive belonging and attachment to primary caregivers may yield helpful insights if we examine it more closely. Recovery from unhealed childhood trauma in later life requires some understanding of the dynamic of recovery in a healthy and supportive context.

With children who have a sense of belonging and who feel secure and valued, relationships with their primary caregivers are marked by shared identity, open exchange of feelings, and unconditional trust. These three, in a manner of speaking, are extensions of the womb.

A feeling of shared identity anchors the self in its move toward independence and autonomy. A sense of belonging is more than a feeling of attachment. It is a sense of one's own self as defined by another or others. Shared identity is a creative space with boundaries which are flexible and fluid, but always intact.

It is precisely this sense of shared identity that is depicted by the biblical expression identifying the Hebrew people as the "children of Israel." The designation of humans as "children of God" carries the same sense of shared identity. Humans are not mere specimens of a race, or individuated members of a species, they are created, "in the image and likeness of God" (Genesis 1:26-27). After several years of companionship and shared life, Jesus said to his disciples: "I do not call you servants any longer, because the servant does not know what the master is doing; but I have called you friends, because I have made known to you everything that I have heard from my father" (John 15:15).

A sense of shared identity is essential to the health and growth of the self.

An open exchange of feelings is the second characteristic of the child's experience of belonging. Feelings are the core of the self and as such are intensely personal and private. Feelings, by themselves, tend to isolate us from others, not bind us to others. Feelings which are only expressed but not exchanged, violate the self's sense of integrity and threaten the self's feeling of shared identity. Resistance to expression of feeling is not a sign of personal dysfunction as much as it is an indicator of a dysfunctional relationship where there is no exchange of feelings and little shared identity.

Merely expressing one's feelings does not create effective relationships, but can, in fact, lead to just the opposite. When I can no longer keep from expressing my feelings, I feel as if I have exposed my inner self, not a comfortable feeling. Self-exposure is avoided by the healthy self but, paradoxically, becomes a means of self-expression for the isolated and lonely self. Exhibitionism is a desperate attempt to make contact at the public level when there is no exchange of feelings at the personal level.

The relationship between God and Israel was marked by an intense exchange of feelings. The divine pathos is expressed by the prophets as both anger and compassion, both suffering and joy.

> When Israel was a child, I loved him, and out of Egypt I called my son.... Yet it was I who taught Ephraim to walk, I took them up in my arms; but they did not know that I healed them. I led with the cords of human kindness, with bands of love. I was to them like those who lift

infants to their cheeks. I bent down to them and fed
them....How can I give you up, Ephraim? How can I
hand you over, O Israel?...My heart recoils within me;
my compassion grows warm and tender;...(Hosea 11:1,
3-4; 8).[2]

In the presence of the grieving sisters of Lazarus, Jesus
openly wept at the tomb where the dead man lay (John
11:35). With his disciples, Jesus freely shared his feelings
as he enabled them to share theirs. In his time of greatest
distress, he kept three of his disciples "within a stone's
throw" so that they could hear his emotional expressions of
fear and anguish (Luke 22:41-44).

When feelings are exchanged between the child and the
caregiver, a passageway is created for the recovery of
shared identity when we feel hurt, abandoned, or unloved.

Unconditional trust is the third characteristic of the
child's experience of belonging. The instinctive fear of
strangers and the compulsive clinging to a caregiver
appears normally at around the eighth or ninth month in a
child's development. This can become a bother to parents
and cause a feeling of rejection to the grandparent whose
visits are marked by periods of separation! The child's distrust of strangers is caused by the building of trust between
the child and the caregiver through the experience of
shared identity and the exchange of feelings. Those who
have not crossed the portal of shared feelings and experienced shared identity are felt to be strangers, even though
they may have a familiar face. This explains why familiar-
ity alone does not always lead to trust, and why even in
marriage and extended family, there may be awkwardness
and the inability to express feelings.

Unconditional trust must be developed before there can

be conditional trust. Children can learn to limit the amount of trust they place in others and in their own experiments with life. But unconditional trust must first of all be experienced as a reality of the self's existence in the world before conditional trust can be practiced with wisdom.

Theodore Roszak eloquently makes this point when he says:

> We meet as strangers, each carrying a mystery within us. I cannot say who you are; I may never know you completely. But I trust that you are a person in your own right, possessed of a beauty and value that are the world's richest resources. So I make this promise to you; I will impose no identities upon you, but will invite you to become yourself, without shame or fear. I will defend your right to find authentic vocation. For as long as your search takes, you have my loyalty.[3]

These three characteristics—shared identity, exchange of feelings, and unconditional trust—are the environment of the adaptable child who is able to recover quickly from the childhood traumas of everyday life.

For many, however, like Ann earlier in this book, the childhood trauma of abandonment by her mother was not healed. She is now in the recovery process from unhealed childhood trauma. Others, who have suffered from neglect and abuse in their childhood live with unresolved and often unacknowledged feelings caused by these traumatic experiences. For those of us who seek recovery in this area, the process is difficult but not impossible.

Recovery from Unhealed Childhood Trauma

At the outset, it must be made clear that recovery is a normal and necessary part of the growth and development of the self. Recovery is not simply a therapeutic process or technique for those who are dysfunctional in some area of life. Recovery is the normal work of the self in adapting to the experiences of life, integrating both negative and positive feelings into a coherent and credible narrative. All recovery is thus based on the dynamic of self-recovery.

Therapeutic aid may well be brought in to assist the process of self-recovery, but recovery is a normal process and function of the life of the self. When therapy is effective it is because it unlocks, supports and assists the process of self-recovery.

The three characteristics of the self's experience of belonging in a secure and safe environment of care—shared self-identity, exchange of feelings, and unconditional trust—are the components of the process of recovery from unhealed childhood trauma. These positive dynamics of recovery can be seen at work in normal recovery when we examine a typical case.

I watch my two-year-old grandson as he plays. Suddenly, his three-year-old brother reaches out to grab the toy car with which he is playing and in order to take it pushes the two-year-old to the side. In being pushed aside, the one falls and hits his head against the coffee table. I watch attentively. Is he badly hurt? He does not immediately cry, though his lower lip pouts and he looks stunned and uncertain.

I continue to watch him. Suddenly he catches my eye and I hold out my arms. Before he comes toward me he is now beginning to cry. I take him in my arms and let the sobs subside. I ask him where it hurts so that I can kiss the spot. The tears are gone. He lingers for a few minutes in my arms, and then just as suddenly slides down and picks up a toy with a smile on his face and begins to play. The trauma is over.

I replay the incident in my mind, with a "freeze-frame" approach at the critical points.

At the point of impact, when the toy is roughly taken and the physical hurt is felt, the boy appears to be momentarily stunned and disoriented. His reaction is like one who feels isolated, as though he has been torn from his place in a safe and familiar world. I remember my own feelings when treated harshly by others and when I experience intense physical pain. A sense of isolation occurs, a feeling of being cut off from others, even those who are closest to me.

Pain, whether physical or emotional, causes a feeling of isolation, of being cut off from some kind of life-support system. The boy experiences the shock of this isolation. This is the first impact of trauma upon the self, at once brutal and devastating. But the significant thing is that it does not immediately bring about the tears.

I advance to the next "freeze-frame." It is the moment in which he recognizes me and sees that I am aware of him. This is when the tears come. What do we make of this?

I recall the process of recovery. Shared identity leads to exchange of feelings. In the boy's sense of devastation and isolation, feelings are encapsulated within the panic-stricken self. The feelings caused by physical pain and the rough treatment by his brother are sucked into the vortex of his feelings of abandonment and isolation. It is *these* feelings which are the key to his recovery.

The recognition of my face and the invitation of my arms touches the self of the boy and becomes a reminder of shared identity. In my arms he will recover the self that has been broken off and abandoned. In turning toward me the tears begin to come. The crying is not so much from the pain but from the need to be heard—to be recognized and loved and cared for.

In my arms, an exchange of feelings occurs. I absorb his feelings of hurt, frustration and isolation. In exchange, I give him my feelings of sympathy, tenderness, and love.

I can resist crying when hurt or feeling abandoned, but not when someone expresses concern and sympathy. Am I unique in this? Is it not true that we are most vulnerable at the level of our feelings when there is some genuine exchange of feeling taking place?

I move to the next "freeze-frame." Now he is in my arms. The physical pain has subsided. The exchange of feelings has taken place. But he tarries a bit, as if to savor the moment. And what is this moment? It is the recovery of the feeling of unconditional trust. He is "recharging" his batteries, so to speak. The shared identity and exchange of feelings has done its work.

The feeling of unconditional trust is when we know that "recovery" has taken place. An exchange of feelings is the passageway to this shared identity. Shared identity is the basis for unconditional trust. This is recovery from the normal experience of childhood trauma.

When child trauma is experienced as rejection, abuse, or other results of a dysfunctional family system, the trauma goes beyond the normal occurrences described above. When these traumas go unhealed, they contribute to adult dysfunctional patterns and it is from these experiences that we need to seek recovery.

The case of Ann, again, presents us with just such an instance. Abandoned by her mother, the three components of normal recovery from childhood trauma did not occur. She experienced the trauma of isolation, found no place for an exchange of feelings, and failed to experience unconditional trust.

Without knowing the facts of her mother's abandonment, her own capacity to function effectively in the primary relationships of her adult life was impaired.

The recovery process for Ann began by approaching the passageway of the exchange of feelings. The child in her was still standing in painful isolation and disorientation. These were present feelings, of course, for feelings are timeless and always contemporary with the self. The metaphor of the child serves to recover the *place* within her self where those feelings lie buried and inaccessible.

For a child to survive in the case of abandonment, neglect or abuse, the negative feelings must be split off and not expressed. Failing to receive the minimal love and positive support needed, the child undertakes to maintain the relation through her own devices. By performing well and conforming to the expectations of the adults around her, she earns acceptance and achieves the status of belonging.

Growing into an adult, this child, like Ann, becomes reasonably adept at the level of social exchange but not at the level of feeling exchange. She experiences peer group acceptance, enters into marriage, and becomes a member of a church. The unhealed trauma of her early abandonment causes occasional periods of depression and an unfulfilling sexual relationship with her husband. Receiving prescription drugs from her physician to alleviate a variety of vague symptoms of stress and fatigue, she begins a borderline chemical dependency.

The facade of well-being and happiness which she has maintained through the years comes crashing down with the revelation from her father that her mother had not died in childbirth, but had abandoned her a year later. No longer can she contain her feelings. They are expressed in highly inappropriate and hurtful ways to both husband and children.

Her recovery process begins with a discussion of these feelings in a traditional therapeutic relationship. Ann is referred to a therapist who enables her to experience a safe and non-threatening environment in which her feelings can be expressed. From the therapist she receives positive feelings of her own value and worth as a person. Ann enters group therapy where she discovers the boundaries of shared identity, a creative space where she has arms to hold her when she cries and faces to look at when she feels scared and alone again.

A few months later, after Ann's therapy began, I asked her how the recovery process was going. She said, "You know, for the first time in my life I am experiencing a relationship with people that I am learning to trust. I couldn't really trust anyone before, but now I am building a capacity to give and receive trust. In our group, we are in a bonding process where we share an intention to support and care for each other. I trust these people to be there for me."

I knew then that she was on her way to recovery. For unconditional trust is the sign that the exchange of feelings and shared identity has done its work.

"So you have no more bad days?" I asked, with a question mark in my voice. "Oh I still do," she responded quickly. "I have some relapses, but I guess that's part of recovery."

"Yes," I replied. "You can only have a relapse when you are in recovery. You are no longer a child, and it will take some time for the fresh discovery of old pain to be absorbed and transformed."

I shared with her the poem by C. S. Lewis, written after the crushing blow he suffered in the loss of his wife, in which he pays testimony to the deep hold which traumatic pain has upon the self.

RELAPSE

Out of the wound we pluck
The shrapnel. Thorns we squeeze
Out of the hand. Even poison forth we suck,
And after pain have ease.

But images that grow
Within the soul have life
Like cancer and, often cut, live on below
The deepest of the knife,

Waiting their time to shoot
At some defenseless hour
Their poison, unimpaired, at the heart's root,
And, like a golden shower,

Unanswerably sweet,
Bright with returning guilt,
Fatally in a moment's time defeat
Our brazen towers long-built,

And all our former pain
And all our surgeon's care
Is lost, and all the unbearable (in vain
Borne once) is still to bear.[4]

Ann will tell you that she is still in recovery. Her relapses are less frequent and her circle of unconditional trust is growing to the point where she can begin to trust in limited and conditional ways. Because she has discovered a place of shared identity, exchange of feelings, and unconditional trust, she has moved from therapeutic recovery to normal recovery.

Normal recovery is daily self-care. Normal recovery is, as the Bible says, to be angry where appropriate, but not let the sun go down on your wrath (Ephesians 4:25). Normal self-recovery is to get up when we hit our head against the coffee table and look for someone whose arms are always extended out to us.

"Come to me," said Jesus, "all you that are weary and are carrying heavy burdens, and I will give you rest. Take my yoke upon you, and learn from me; for I am gentle and humble in heart, and you will find rest for your souls. For my yoke is easy, and my burden is light" (Matthew 11:28).

The child in us knows where to go when God holds out his arms.

CHAPTER TEN

Recovering from Abusive Relationships

"You always hurt the one you love," is an adage that may have had its origin in a song, but it is a painful reality for many abused children and spouses in our contemporary homes.

The incidence of abusive behavior is shocking and sobering. We can account for violence in the streets by attributing such actions to persons who have no concern for the rights of others. I do not feel betrayed if a stranger assaults me. I may suffer injury and experience emotional trauma, but I am not hurt nearly so much as I would be if one who claims to love me causes the injury and the trauma.

The fact that intimate social relationships are high risk situations for abuse demands closer analysis. There appears to be some correlation between intimacy and abusive relationships. If so, we need to discover the inner dynamics of such a correlation and attempt to develop preventative methods of intervention, as well as suggest a process of recovery from these abusive relationships.

What Constitutes Abuse?

Abusive behavior within the family is different from all other forms of violence in that it has its highest potential for injury where there is the greatest potential for intimacy and love. The most dangerous place for a child in our society is in the home, according to child molestation and abuse statistics. The most dangerous place for a woman is not on the streets, but in some form of intimate relationship with a man.[1]

A published report by the American Medical Association reveals that one out of every four women in the United States experiences some form of abuse from a man she lives with or to whom she is related. One-third of all women who arrive at doctors' offices or hospitals seeking emergency treatment, and up to one-quarter of all those seeking prenatal care are victims of domestic violence. Each year, four million women are severely assaulted by their current or former partner. More than half of female murder victims are slain by their husband or boyfriend.[2]

. Our first thought on hearing this is to suppose that it is the absence of love in the context of domestic and family intimacy which accounts for such abuse. If adults really loved their children and if adults really loved each other, it would be impossible for abusive behavior to occur. Wrong. Family violence is not due to the absence of love, for love and violence can coexist in primary relationships where persons are the most vulnerable.

Sociologists Richard Gelles and Murray Straus say "That violence and love can actually coexist in families is perhaps the most insidious aspect of intimate violence because it means that, unlike violence in the streets, we are tied to abusers by the bonds of love, attachment, and affection."[3]

Nor can we attribute acts of violence between persons who live together to some form of mental derangement, as though "normal" persons would never resort to such actions. The fact is, as Gelles and Straus report, "only about ten percent of abusive incidents are caused by mental illness. The remaining ninety percent are not amenable to psychological explanation."[4] The majority of persons who commit family violence are normal persons as measured by accepted societal standards. This means that psychiatric treatment will not ordinarily prove effective in reducing the incidence of this kind of abusive behavior.

Does this suggest, then, that there is a range of normal physical force that should be expected and tolerated in these domestic settings? Is it normal for parents to use physical force in disciplining a child, such as spanking or other forms of forcible punishment? Do not people who love each other often express their anger and frustration through harsh words and even pushing and shoving? Should we make allowance for force that is normal but which is not abusive?

The distinction between normal and abusive force, once used to distinguish between the force used in attempts to discipline as against violence which causes injury no longer has credibility among many sociologists.[5] For this reason, I prefer to speak of abusive relationships whether physical force is used or not. The use of physical means to exercise control over another can become a more overt form of abuse that is already taking place through the violation of another person's dignity and personal space.

We should also be aware of the fact that, while incidents of physical abuse may appear to be isolated and unconnected, a deeper pattern of abuse often underlies isolated incidents. One case of domestic violence may be closely connected to other acts of violence or abuse in the home. Studies have shown that child abuse incidents are higher in homes where there is spouse abuse.[6]

Abuse is always, to some degree, a violation of the other person. Because we have tended to associate violence with the use of physical force resulting in physical harm, other abuse often goes undetected and unacknowledged.

Abuse as a Violation of Personhood

Whenever abuse occurs in a relationship there is a violation of the personal being of one person by another. The risk of abuse is greater where persons are in primary relationships where intimate contact is experienced. This accounts for the high incidence of abuse between family members.

Primary relationships tend to be intimate, personal and sensitive. Secondary relationships tend to be more functional, impersonal, and task-oriented.

The checkout person at the supermarket may be friendly, but basically functions in a secondary relationship. If this person is impersonal and quite insensitive to my feelings on a particular day, I may feel slighted, but this is at a different level than abuse from a person upon whom I am dependent for my sense of personal well-being. When secondary types of relationships are abusive, we become angry at being treated impersonally or unjustly, but we are sufficiently insulated against this type of abuse so as not to be deeply hurt or injured by it.

We seem to have an instinctive sense of when we are moving out of primary relationships into secondary ones when we leave the company of a good friend to stand in line at the Department of Motor Vehicles! While there *is* a sense of abuse when confronted by the impersonal nature of a bureaucracy, it is quite different from the same treatment by one who professes to love and care for us.

Primary relationships carry an implicit promise of mutual care, respect and trust. It is only on the basis of such qualities in the relationship that we risk ourselves to the intimacy of sharing our thoughts, personal space, and physical touch. When we form such relationships we expect to feel safe, free to respond, and nurtured in our own need for self-care. The moment that we no longer feel safe or free to respond, a violation has occurred, and abuse has begun.

When Don and Sally came to me for premarital counseling, we began the usual series of tests and discussions which focused on compatibility and role relationships in marriage. After a few weeks, Sally asked for an appointment to discuss a personal and private matter.

"Maybe I shouldn't be concerned," she began, "but I have felt increasingly uncomfortable with certain aspects of our relationship. Don seems to expect me to respond at times with signs of physical affection which I feel are inappropriate. If I do not respond, he sulks and will not call me for several days. Sometimes, this goes on for a week or more, until I call him and apologize. If I respond to him the way he wants me to, then everything is really fine between us."

As we talked, it became clear that there were other patterns in their relationship which exhibited Don's need to control her. He wanted her to dress in certain ways when they went out. If she did not comply, he would get angry and punish her by not taking her out.

"I really love him," she told me, "and I feel that he loves me. Maybe after we are married he will feel more secure and I will have more freedom to respond and please him."

What Sally revealed was a pattern of abusive behavior under the guise of rather typical dating patterns in our culture. My counseling with them immediately moved into this area. Don and Sally were headed for a potentially abusive marriage. The seeds of abuse and violence were already being sown and were far from harmless personality quirks and lack of social skills.

The beginning of abuse in a relationship may be so imperceptible that it is like the proverbial story of the frog in the kettle. When the water at first is the same temperature as the frog, there is no discomfort. As the water is gradually increased in temperature, the frog makes adjustments to the change until finally, when the water reaches its boiling point, it is too late to jump out!

Sally was ready to make adjustments to the behavior of Don for the sake of keeping a loving relationship. What she did not realize is that the water was already beginning to boil.

The Continuum of Abusive Relationships

Abuse begins in a relationship when almost imperceptible lines are crossed . . . where what was once safe, nurturing, and empowering becomes oppressive, coercive, and demanding. Sally feels uncomfortable in her relationship with Don, but is powerless to express these feelings for fear of breaking the relationship. Sally feels inadequate to set boundaries based on what she perceives to be appropriate responses. Don is unaware of her boundaries because they are unexpressed and because of his own need to find reassurance by controlling her response to him.

When I placed the positive and negative qualities of a relationship on a continuum and asked Sally to indicate where she would place herself in her relationship with Don, she immediately saw the pattern of abuse which was beginning. This is what the diagram looked like:

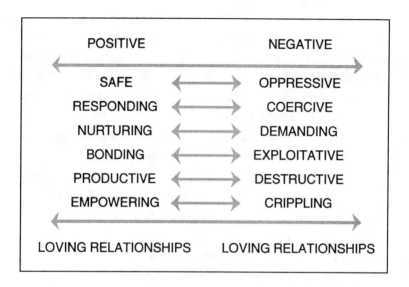

While Sally continued to feel deeply bonded with Don and did not feel that the relationship with him was destructive and crippling, she did not feel responsive and nurturing. She felt coerced to respond in many cases and felt that his demands upon her left her feeling uncared for. To some degree she also felt oppressed and realized that she also felt vulnerable at the physical level and not completely safe.

When Sally placed herself on each of these continuums as to how she felt about her relationship with Don, she became aware that the relationship was already moving from positive to negative and from loving to abusive. The next step was to discuss this with both Don and Sally, using the diagram to help Don see precisely what her feelings were in regard to his demands upon her.

It was a painful and difficult experience for Don. In the end, however, it proved to be an effective intervention into the abusive tendencies in their relationship. When Don was asked to indicate on each continuum where his feelings were in regard to Sally's relationship with him, it became apparent that he too felt some level of coercion from Sally and, most important, felt disempowered and somewhat crippled by her assertive role in making decisions concerning her career without consulting him. It was somewhat of a shock for Sally to discover that Don also felt abused in the relationship!

As they began to communicate honestly about their feelings through use of the diagram, their relationship with each other and the boundaries of each became clearer. They discovered a means to conduct a personal audit with regard to these feelings and boundaries while maintaining a commitment to be open to each other's feelings and the integrity of each other's boundaries.

In pastoral counseling I have discovered that teenage dating patterns reveal tendencies toward abusive behavior under the sanction of accepted cultural roles in the relationship. Because men are often assumed to have the responsibility for initiating a relationship, women often feel a violation of personal integrity, disempowered, and helpless when confronted with demands for greater intimacy. Fearing rejection and possibly the loss of the relationship, the woman may feel pressured to respond. At this moment, the relationship has become oppressive, coercive, and demanding.

Men are invariably shocked and defensive when this is pointed out to them. Nor are women always ready to acknowledge this as abusive behavior. Only after marriage, in many cases, does the more overt abuse become apparent in the form of economic, emotional, and physical forms of oppression and coercion.

In abusive relationships, there may be a sense of personal inadequacy on the part of both the offender and the victim. In this case, the victim lacks the self-worth and ego strength to set boundaries or, as may well be necessary in some cases, to terminate the relationship as the first step in self-recovery from the abusive situation. This may explain why victims of abuse often find it difficult to report it or, even when reported, to terminate the relationship.

The recent focus on sexual harassment in the workplace points to the same continuum of abuse. Men are often totally unaware of what constitutes sexual harassment because of the cultural pattern of male sexuality which dissociates intimacy from physical sexuality. When the criteria of what constitutes abusive behavior are applied, as defined above, the issue is not so much the sexual aspect of the relationship but the issues of gender and power.

The power dynamics of the workplace tend to place women at a disadvantage with regard to equal opportunity and recognition. When sexual harassment becomes the particular form of oppression, coercion, and exploitation, the power differential is gender-oriented and sexually contrived. When sexual harassment is seen as a form of abusive relationship, it can better be understood and dealt with. A model for the prevention of abuse and domestic violence begins with a process of self-recovery where the boundaries of what constitutes abuse in personal and professional relationships become clear.

Where abuse has occurred or is occurring, the one who is abused needs to make the move toward recovery. Because abuse is often hidden and the victim often powerless, recovery cannot begin until the secret is told. Short of physical violence attracting the attention of others, the victim of abuse often suffers secretly and silently.

Breaking the secret of abuse is difficult for two reasons:
First, the devastation wrought by abusive relationships is so deep and pervasive that the incidents of abuse are often repressed and hidden from conscious memory. Children

who have been physically or sexually abused often repress memory of these incidents as a means of survival. This can cause a splitting of the self and apparently, in some extreme cases, result in what psychologists identify as Multiple Personality Syndrome.

Second, survival in a relationship upon which one is dependent, as a child upon a caregiver, or a marriage partner upon a spouse, may require keeping the abuse a secret for fear of retaliation or loss of one's means of livelihood.

Finally, because the type of abuse which occurs in a relationship with others violates the capacity of the self to be open and trustful of others, recovery requires a renewal of the self through relationships which are safe and renewing.[7]

Recovering from Abuse: A Healing of the Spirit

Resources for recovery from the physical and psychological trauma of abuse are abundant and readily available. This chapter focuses on the recovery of the self's spiritual core of self-care and self-affirmation. The nature of abuse which occurs in personal relationships is a form of violence against the self's spirit leaving an invisible wound which time alone will not heal.

To suffer abuse is not only to experience psychological trauma, but spiritual desecration. The term "desecration" implies the violation of something sacred, an intrusion upon that which is holy. In suffering sustained abuse, the self is not only injured so as to require healing, it suffers a violation for which only a restoration of the self's innate sense of spiritual integrity will suffice. This is what makes abuse in the context of intimacy so destructive and devastating.

The psychological effects of trauma and abuse may sometimes be removed or alleviated through therapy. Recovery from abuse always involves a restoration of emotional and mental health. But the desecration of the self's spirit requires a spiritual therapy which renews and restores health and wholeness to the spirit.

Trusting another person to care for us as we would care for ourselves is an openness of the spirit to the spirit of another. Trust is the sacred key given to another by which access to one's own secret self may be unlocked. Violation of this trust is unlawful entry into the sacred chamber of the self, a desecration of that which is most holy, for it is a gift of God.

The human self, as explained in Chapter Two, has a spiritual core that is created in the image and likeness of God, who is Spirit and life. While our passions move us, it is spirit that gives the self direction and hope. Feelings are the core of emotion, spirit is the core and center of the self. Human feelings are not possible without spirit. Feelings may be hurt, but spirit is quenched.

The Old Testament scholar, Abraham Heschel tells us "Spirit implies the sense of sharing a supreme superindividual power, will or wisdom. In emotion, we are conscious of its being our emotion; in the state of being filled with spirit, we are conscious of joining, sharing or receiving 'spirit from above' (Isa. 32:15)."[8]

The biblical story of Creation depicts the formation of the first humans by saying, "The Lord God formed man from the dust of the ground, and breathed into his nostrils the breath of life; and the man became a living being" (Gen. 2:7). Human life is inspired life! To inspire is to "give spirit," to "quicken spirit."

Following His death, the disciples of Jesus were inconsolable, though they each had similar emotions of discouragement and despair. Suddenly, they experienced Jesus Himself amidst them, and He "breathed on them and said to them, 'Receive the Holy Spirit'"(John 20:22). They not only experienced a radical shift in their emotions, they were touched in their own spirit and inspired by the Spirit of God. This inspiration gave rise to an emotional strength which empowered them to undertake incredible tasks, to endure incredible sufferings, and to experience incredible joy and hope.

The emotional center of the self is located in the spirit, not in the tormenting events of the past nor in the traumatic events of the present. The self has its source in spirit, and therefore has a center which also points to a destiny. Where this spiritual center has suffered molestation and violation, nothing less than a loving and gracious spirit can bring recovery. The inspiration of the Spirit of God is a practical guide to self-recovery by touching the human spirit at the core, and empowering it to recover the new life that the Spirit of God graciously gives.

I have suggested that abuse desecrates the spirit of the self. Abuse is unlawful entry into the sacred chamber of the spirit, a violation of the self's own sense of holiness. The spirit of the self is holy as it has virtue—it is essentially good; as it has value—it is of inestimable worth; as it has vision—it sees its own virtue and value reflected in the eyes of love.

The recovery of virtue. No one needs to teach a child that he possesses an essential goodness. This does not mean that the child is good in everything, but that even in its disposition and actions which are self-centered and harmful to others, it is essentially good. Virtue is not an acquired character through the practice of moral disciplines, but the sense of one's own goodness as a spiritual being, albeit an imperfect one! The Bible tells us that we are born with the defect of selfish and sinful inclinations and that the grace of God is needed to redeem us from such. That is true, but virtue is the goodness of the spirit given to us by God in our creation, not the result of our own good behavior! The fact that we need the grace of God to discover and uncover our God-created goodness does not deny that goodness but rather, esteems it. My children were never perfect, but they were always good. That is, by virtue of their being my children they were essentially good!

Abuse desecrates this innate sense of goodness. The child who is sexually abused by a caregiver begins to feel that he or she must be bad to deserve such treatment. After all, the caregiver is the only source of love and life. If one thinks that one is bad, that accounts for the bad thing that is happening.

A spouse who is abused by the one who provides the "good" things necessary for life, begins to feel that she or he must be a bad person to deserve such punishment. When one who has been repeatedly abused by a spouse becomes compliant and obedient, the abuser may say, "You have been good for several days now. I haven't had to punish you for a long time." This reinforces the feeling of the abused person as not really being good and as deserving the abuse.

Abuse desecrates the spirit by robbing the person of a sense of inward goodness. When the door to the self's sacred chamber of essential goodness has been broken through and every last shred of dignity and decency stripped away, abuse has done its work. The victim has become a slave, living off the few crumbs of affection tossed indiscriminately on the floor.

I mentioned earlier the splitting effect which abuse has upon the self. The sense of good can be split from the sense of being bad. The good self becomes compliant, subservient, and even religious, out of fear of punishment. The bad self takes the blame for all of the negative things that happen, including the abuse as deserved punishment. There can be no virtue in this. The spirit is quenched, for it cannot live in the false sense of goodness nor in the despair of badness.

Virtue is not the good side of the self as opposed to the bad, but the integration of the self in such a way that the spirit recovers its sense of being holy and not defiled. The Bible speaks of both "unclean" and "holy" spirits, and both are aptly named! To live as though one's own spirit is "unclean" is to be desecrated at the very core of the self. The picture of "unclean spirits" invading a person and being driven out, as with the case of King Saul (1 Samuel 16), vividly portrays the condition of one whose own spirit has become defiled. David, after confessing to his own immoral actions and receiving God's grace and forgiveness, said, "...do not take your holy spirit from me. Restore me to the joy of your salvation, and sustain in me a willing spirit" (Psalm 51:11, 12).

Virtue is recovered when our desecrated and devastated spirits are renewed in holiness and goodness by the Spirit and grace of God. We are in recovery when we are able to affirm our own essential goodness as bearers of God's good spirit, created in his image and likeness. This is the spiritual work of healing that is necessary to recovery from abuse.

We are in the place of spiritual recovery when we are with people whose own spirits are full of virtue. These people are open to God's Spirit through worship, prayer and shared life.

The recovery of value. Abuse not only desecrates the spirit of the self in violating its virtue, but in destroying its value. The victim of abuse, especially sexual abuse, can come to feel that one is "damaged goods." The abuser retains power over the victim by sending messages like this: "If you didn't have me, you wouldn't have anybody. Who would want you!"

Where virtue has to do with the essential goodness of the self, a quality like holiness, a sacred sense of the self, value has to do with the worth of the self, particularly to others. Virtue is something that the self is meant to possess as an innate quality of life. Value is a sense of the self's worth to others.

Abuse desecrates the spirit by devaluing the self as contemptible and undesirable by others. If one is made to feel worthless, then the abuser has power over the victim by pretending to give value and worth, even though it is not deserved. The abuser will stress how important and necessary the victim is to the abuser, giving the impression that the only source of value for the victim is to be found in relationship to the abuser.

The victim is thus placed in a double bind. Being made to feel worthless by the abuse, the victim looks to the abuser as the only one who seems to offer worth. In a strange and terribly twisted way, the victim's only value is found in meeting the abuser's need for someone to abuse!

When others attempt to intervene and affirm the worth of the victim of abuse as an argument to escape the abuse, the evidence of the abuse is a more powerful witness to the worthlessness of the self than the desperate entreaty of friends.

Abuse can cause one to lose the capacity to feel valued by non-abusive persons. As one woman who suffered from abusive parents and an abusive husband in her first marriage told me, "I did not know how to live without pain. It did not seem normal." Feeling worthless can become a normal feeling for one who has suffered from abuse.

Recovery from the desecration of abuse to the spirit begins when the value of the self can be affirmed in such a way that it can be believed. We must remember that the negative value of worthlessness is created through actions which are abusive. This means that the value of having personal worth cannot be communicated through words alone, but through actions and relationships which are non-abusive.

The apostle Paul wrote a brief letter to his friend Philemon, which later found its way into the New Testament canon. In this letter, Paul tells Philemon that Onesimus, a slave of Philemon, is being sent back. We do not know whether Onesimus had been sent by Philemon to serve Paul or had run away and was now being returned. In any event, Paul found Onesimus of great value to him, and in sending him back, said, "Formerly he was useless to you, but now he is indeed useful both to you and to me" (Philemon 11). The Greek name, Onesimus, means useful, or beneficial. Paul's play on words conveys the deeper significance of the fact that Philemon is now to view his former slave in an entirely different light. Onesimus discovered his true worth in serving Paul, who now asks Philemon to treat his slave as a brother.

The metaphor of slavery is an apt one with regard to an abusive relationship. Abuse makes slaves of those who are abused, treating them as having worth only as objects to be used for the abuser's own gratification. Recovery from abuse is to move out of the abuser's power of deception into the truth and freedom of one's own worth and value. Abuse desecrates the spirit in the victim by perpetrating the lie that the victim is worthless except as a slave.

Jesus of Nazareth, who treated all persons as having unique value, said, "The truth will make you free" (John 15: 32). "The slave does not have a permanent place in the household; the son has a place there forever. So if the Son makes you free, you will be free indeed" (John 15:35-36).

We are in the place of recovery when we accept the love and care of others as signs of our own worth, not merely as credit to their own goodness. We know that recovery is taking place when we feel the spirit within us responds to the spirit of truth and love in others who value their own life. We can trust that spirit, but it is the Spirit of God leading us out of bondage into glorious liberty as children of God.

The recovery of vision. The spirit of the self is holy as it has virtue—it is essentially good; as it has value—it is of inestimable worth; as it has vision—it sees its own virtue and value reflected in the eyes of love.

Virtue and value have no power in recovery until they are believed to be true by one's own self. Ultimately, recovery is self-recovery. That is, the self must become the self that it really is despite the violation and abuse which has taken place.

For all of the pain which the human spirit often must endure, it is indestructible. It can be bruised and broken, but not demolished. The terrible power of abuse is not that it can destroy the human spirit, but that it can blind it to its own virtue and value. When the vision of the self is obscured, it has lost its power of recovery. This vision must be restored.

"The eye is the lamp of the body," said Jesus. "So, if your eye is healthy, your whole body will be full of light; but if your eye is unhealthy, your whole body will be full of darkness. If then the light in you is darkness, how great is the darkness!" (Matthew 6:22-23).

Abuse desecrates the human spirit by distorting the vision which the self has of its own virtue and value. Recovery involves the healing of this vision in order that new boundaries can be set and the inner life consecrated once more as good and worthy of care.

Vision is a metaphor which suggests several aspects of recovery. Restored vision may require the right amount of light, a corrective lens, and a point of view.

How can we acquire these?

First, we need to have the right amount of light in order to have clear vision. The power of abuse is its secrecy. When the secret of abuse is revealed, light has entered into darkness. In some cases, early childhood abuse has become a secret even to the self. Consultation with a qualified therapist can often uncover those secrets and shed light upon the abuse which has caused us to devalue ourselves. Where abuse is ongoing and recognized, it must be exposed to the light by breaking its secret.

It is the appropriate amount and kind of light that needs to be shed on the abusive situation. Too much light, or light of the wrong kind, can cause its own distortion of vision. Unfortunately, some have disclosed abuse to persons who were themselves threatened by this revelation and whose reaction was one of denial, or even blame. In some cases, disclosure of abuse has caused some to suggest spiritual platitudes as a means of giving value to the suffering caused by abuse without making an intervention and stopping the abuse.

There are twelve-step programs available in almost every city. These are made up of people who themselves are in recovery and often can provide a place with sufficient light to expose the evil of abuse while also shielding the self from the glare of overexposure.

Next, we need to have an eye examination! When we have problems with our eyesight, we go to a specialist who locates the distortion and prescribes a corrective lens. When we have been the victim of abuse we need to go to specialists in nonabusive love and care. More than that, we need to ask them to conduct an eye examination by asking us what we see when we take a good look at ourselves. We need to trust their diagnosis in order to correct our self-vision.

Even as an ophthalmologist may write out a prescription for a lens that corrects our vision, we need a written prescription from those who have a more accurate vision of our own virtue and value than we do. It is not that others have not been saying these words to us, but that we have not believed them. We have trusted our own distorted vision of ourselves more than theirs. The written prescription of those who view us more accurately than we view ourselves can be given the authority of having the truth which will set us free!

Finally, we need a new point of view. It does not help to have a corrected lens and sufficient light if we have no point of view!

When the self has vision, it sees its own virtue and value reflected in the eyes of love. Dr. Judith Herman, M.D., has wisely said, "Recovery can take place only in the context of relationships; it cannot occur in isolation. In her renewed connections with other people, the survivor recreates the psychological faculties that were damaged or deformed by the traumatic experience.... Just as these capabilities are originally formed in relationships with other people, they must be reformed in such relationships."[9]

The point of view for the self is through the eyes of love.

One of the most well-known incidents in the New Testament is the betrayal of Jesus by Judas Iscariot with a kiss. In an imaginary dialogue occurring after this tragic incident that I created between Judas and Jesus, I have Judas finally say, after an extended series of exchanges with Jesus:

"I thought I could see, but I was blind. Through your eyes I see that my life is no longer flat and one-dimensional. The door I closed became transparent. I—I see a different Judas on the other side.

"It's not enough to use my eyes, Judas. I have touched yours so that you may see yourself, and for yourself, that you are my friend."[10]

Recovery is recovery of our own virtue, our own value, and the vision which we have of ourselves through the eyes of love. It is our own vision that finally marks the reality of recovery. This vision is one which the Spirit of God creates in us, and it is one which our own spirit is empowered to see and believe.

CHAPTER ELEVEN

Recovering from Shame and Self-Condemnation

Most everyone walks through a valley of shame now and then. Some of us, however, take a lifelong lease on shame; it is our permanent home. We are shame-bound.... Some of us are so hooked into shame that we are afraid we would be lonely without it.... If we lost our shame, we would not recognize ourselves.[1]

I have received only a few traffic citations over the past 25 years and, while I cannot recall the date, I can remember precisely the details of each incident. I know exactly where my car was stopped by the flashing red light. I can visualize clearly the scene, handing over my driver's license, standing behind the car waiting for the officer to write out the ticket while other cars went speeding by. I remember word for word the brief conversation, and have replayed the tape many times in my mind trying to insert new explanations into the script, sometimes being sarcastic, sometimes humorous.

In each case, I paid the fine immediately and, as far as

the law was concerned, I was no longer guilty and had nothing to fear from any traffic officer, at least with regard to that offense. The receipt which indicated that the fine had been paid in full was my assurance that whatever guilt I had incurred for the violation had been removed.

Why then was I unable to erase the incident from my mind and let go of the emotions which the incident produced? I have attempted in vain to recall other experiences of joy and pleasure from the past which must have been deeply moving at the time but which mingle now with positive aspects of the self to produce wholeness of life. My guess is that the feelings of pleasure were integrated into the healthy core of the self. The feelings of humiliation and embarrassment when "caught in the act" have their own secret places in the psychic jungle.

The Feeling of Shame is a Powerful Secret

As I have reflected on the growing literature on shame and its effect on the self, I think that I understand more clearly what happened to me. I was startled to discover that I carried deep within me such a vivid recollection of the incidents and, in particular, the same sensations and feelings I had at the time. I wondered why incidents like these had such power virtually to burn into my psyche the details of the incident as well as the feelings I experienced. I only have to recall each incident to experience once again the feelings of humiliation at being caught, exposed to the merciless gaze of the other motorists and in some cases, curious bystanders.

I also discovered that my pattern was never to disclose the incident to others and to act as though it had never happened. While it was a matter of public record for strangers to look at, it was also a secret to be kept from those whose affirmation I valued the most. There was nothing to fear from the law, but the possibility of exposure and further humiliation was a fearful threat to my self-esteem.

What I have felt in recalling the traffic violations was the power of shame and its relentless attack upon the vulnerable core of the self. The incidents with the traffic officers penetrated through the normal defenses and found a chink in my psychic armor. A primitive sense of shame, no doubt experienced in childhood, was activated and used this new incident to abuse the self and inflict new wounds, further entrenching itself in the psychic core.

Although trivial, I share my own experience as one that most of us have had, in one form or another. Common to all of us are the feelings of shame when we have felt exposed to the scrutiny of others in a moment of personal failure. What we are concerned about in this chapter is not the general feeling of shame that comes and goes, but the destructive and crippling power of shame that rises up within ourselves, causing us to feel unworthy, disgusting, or rejected. Feelings of self-condemnation often follow instances where shame will not permit us to forgive ourselves nor to accept the forgiveness of others.

Why it is Important to Have a Capacity for Shame

Not all feelings of shame are so destructive to the self. Indeed, the capacity to feel shame seems to be part of the self's maintenance of a healthy sense of limitation and core of humility. To be called "shameless" is to be judged to be without a sense of discrimination as to what is appropriate and what is inappropriate behavior. "In the past the capacity to experience shame was valued," says Robert Karen.

To be capable of shame meant to be modest, as opposed
to exhibitionistic or grandiose, to have character, nobility, honor, discretion. It meant to be respectful of social
standards, of the boundaries of others, of one's own limitations. And, finally, it meant to be respectful of one's
need for privacy.[2]

John Bradshaw also speaks of a healthy and nourishing
shame that keeps us within the boundaries of our own
humanity. This capacity for shame is the foundation for
humility and a source of spirituality.

Shame is a normal human emotion. In fact, it is necessary to have the feeling of shame if one is to be truly
human. Shame is the emotion which gives us permission to be human. Shame tells us of our limits. Shame
keeps us in our human boundaries, letting us know that
we can and will make mistakes, and that we need help.
Our shame tells us that we are not God. Healthy shame
is the psychological foundation of humility. It is the
source of spirituality.[3]

I must confess that it is difficult to think of shame as
normal and even necessary to healthy human existence.
Perhaps this is because we always think of shame as something that we experience as a loss of well-being, as a negative and not a positive feeling.

"There is a nice irony in shame," says Lewis Smedes,
"our feelings of inferiority are a sure sign of our superiori-
ty, and our feelings of unworthiness testify to our great
worth. Only a very noble being can feel shame."[4]

How do we reconcile the fact that to have no capacity
for shame is a sign of inappropriate understanding of the
self yet to experience shame can be negative and even
destructive?

"Our shame tells us that we are not God," says Bradshaw. I do not think that it is shame that tells us that, but the capacity to *sense* shame as a consequence of over-reaching our human limits. The Psalmist says: "O Lord, my heart is not lifted up, my eyes are not raised too high; I do not occupy myself with things too great and too marvelous for me. But I have calmed and quieted my soul, like a weaned child with its mother; my soul is like the weaned child that is with me" (Psalm 131).

The capacity for shame has a spiritual basis, says Smedes. To have a sense of shame is akin to feeling God's presence.

> Spiritual shame may come as a tremor after a close encounter with God, but unhealthy shame is a godless shame. Undeserved shame may come from religion, but it only gets in God's way. Religion without grace can tie shame around our souls like a choke chain and never offer relief. The pain we feel is not even a distant cousin to spiritual shame.[5]

In order to understand the concept of healthy shame, let's take the concept of a limit, or boundary, as Bradshaw suggested.

If a child should attempt to impersonate an adult and attempt some action beyond its ability, it will surely fail and experience shame. If the child has a capacity for shame that could result from such an attempt, she will stop short of the act, and think to herself, "I'm just a child. I am not big enough to do that."

Having a capacity for shame keeps us from doing something that causes us to *be* shamed. It is our capacity for shame that enables us to live comfortably within the boundaries and limits set for us by our capabilities, our relationship with others, and our own sense of dignity and self-worth. A capacity for shame keeps us from violating our dignity by exposing ourselves in such a way as to cause discomfort and offense to others.

Having a capacity for shame keeps us from the foolishness of doing something shameful, as Smedes reminds us. "Our shame may be our best defense against our folly. When it comes down to it, most people do the right thing because they would be ashamed of themselves if they did the wrong thing."[6]

When Shame Becomes a Secret

In the Creation story, the first man and woman "were naked, and were not ashamed" (Gen. 2:25). I have often wondered how they could know that they were not ashamed without some sense of what shame is! I have now concluded that they indeed were created with a capacity for shame and that in the security of that intimacy of relationship with each other, they could be open and exposed to each other without shame actually being felt. Immediately upon overreaching their limits and attempting to "be like God" (3:5), they "knew that they were naked; and they sewed fig leaves together and made loincloths for themselves" (3:7).

At this point, they actually felt shame in the presence of each other and, we assume, in the eyes of God, for they hid themselves from the presence of God in the garden. Adam blamed God for "giving him this woman," and the woman blamed the serpent for beguiling her.

It is one thing to have a keen sense of shame as a possible consequence of an action. It is quite another thing to actually *feel* shame because we have been shamed. Being shamed is a violation of the self which occurs within human interaction. Wherever there is blame there is shame. One continually feeds on the other.

Because of the need to conceal the shameful act, shame is buried as a secret deep within the self. Fear of exposure drives the self deeper into hiding in a desperate attempt to preserve a semblance of decency. When we have been shamed, we put on fig leaves in order to maintain a sense of decorum and acceptability.

It appears that our capacity for shame has lost its innocence and insight. We do not understand the shame that "keeps us within our boundaries," so we cower behind the fig leaves of our own creation. Rather than admitting our mistakes and asking for help, we abuse ourselves with stinging rebuke and merciless condemnation. The fig leaves can hardly be removed before the hurtful shame is removed so that we are able to recover a sense of self-worth and value our humanity.

The experience of being shamed has no motivating power toward health. Once we feel shamed, the capacity for shame no longer functions in a positive sense. Feeling shamed, we are likely to blame and condemn ourselves as though we were guilty of some terrible offense.

The Difference between Shame and Guilt

Guilt has to do with an act which is measured against an objective standard, or against another person. Guilt is the consequence of a violation of this standard. Guilt is removed when one has satisfied the penalty imposed, or is pardoned from the wrong and/or forgiven. The objective nature of the offense is removed from one's record.

The removal of objective guilt may not remove the feeling of shame, which is subjectively rooted in the self's feeling that it has no worth. The confusion between guilt and shame can be the source of much self-condemnation. Often when we continue to feel guilt, we are experiencing shame.

When I paid the traffic ticket, the penalty for violating the law was fulfilled and satisfaction made. There was no longer an objective basis for guilt. Guilt is removed by paying the penalty or seeking pardon.

Shame has to do with a loss to one's identity and being. Long after the guilt has been removed objectively, one can still be caught in the dehumanizing grip of shame. When I feel guilt for having broken a traffic law long after the ticket has been paid, it is really shame that I feel. I experience a loss of personal integrity. My self-worth is threatened. Paying the traffic ticket removes the guilt, but does not restore my sense of personal worth.

Shame does not necessarily disappear even though guilt as an objective offense standing between God and human persons is removed. Shame, as the deeper problem of the self, means that one has suffered loss of being, not merely loss of status. The purpose of divine forgiveness is not only to pardon sin as a legal or objective fault, but to overcome shame which has weakened and destroyed the inner fabric of the self.

When we think of atonement for sin as a removal of guilt we must also understand that it has not produced wholeness and health within until the effects of shame on one's personal being have been overcome.[7]

The continued feeling of shame, Robert Karen, suggests, is a "victimless crime." By that he means that only the self is the victim, and that shame is not an offense against others even though we feel shame in the presence of others.

> If guilt is about behavior that has harmed others, shame is about not being good enough. Shame is often, of course, triggered by something you have done, but in

shame, the way that behavior reflects on you is what counts. Shameful behavior is thus often a victimless crime; and shame itself is less clearly about morality than about conformity, acceptability, or character.[8]

Smedes captures this thought well when he says, "Most of us feel shame not for our too-badness but for our not-good-enoughness. Not measuring up to snuff hurts us more than when we violate a law."[9]

The restoration of personal being and the recovery of a sense of self-worth is a process of restoration through communication and community. Shame isolates, recovery must restore relation. Shame causes inner rage and fury against the self, recovery must disarm that abusive emotion. Shame eats away at the tender and vulnerable core of the self, turning healthy self-love into ritual abuse.

Recovery must stop the self-abuse of shame and release the power of forgiveness and healing into the innermost cell of the self's secrets. While shame is sensed as humiliation before others, it does its vicious work of self-destruction in secret. Recovery is breaking the code of secrecy through which the abuse of shame takes place.

Shame as Self-Abuse

Shame is not an emotion. Shame uses the emotions as instruments of self-punishment and thereby becomes self-abuse. Shame attacks the self, inflicting punishment for the sake of crippling, not to correct. Robert Karen says of shame:

> It *is* crippling, because it contains not just the derisive accusation that one is a wimp, a bully, a runt, or a fag but the further implication that one is at core a deformed

being, fundamentally unlovable and unworthy of membership in the human community. It is the self regarding the self with the withering and unforgiving eye of contempt. And most people are unable to face it. It is too annihilating.[10]

This kind of shame has been called pathological, or toxic shame, to distinguish it from a more benign sense of shame which is intrinsic to the self's awareness of limitations. "Pathological shame is an irrational sense of defectiveness," says Karen, "a feeling not of having crossed to the wrong side of the boundary but of having been born there."[11] This kind of shame is what John Bradshaw calls toxic shame.

> Toxic shame, the shame that binds you, is experienced as the all pervasive sense that I am flawed and defective as a human being. Toxic shame is no longer an emotion that signals our limits, it is a state of being, a core identity. Toxic shame gives you a sense of worthlessness, a sense of failing and falling short as a human being. Toxic shame is a rupture of the self with the self.[12]

To be shame-based is not only to experience a deep sense of personal deficit but to experience oneself as caught in a web of shame that conceals a secret. This secret may lie hidden in one's family of origin. In many families, shame is carried from one generation to another, long after the incident which caused the shame has been forgotten. The secret which led to the original shame dies with a previous generation while the shame continues to be hidden, passed from one generation to the next.

Shame can be transmitted from one generation to another as individuals in the family acquire a sense of unworthiness or inadequacy. This may be disguised as feelings of racial inferiority, social unacceptability, or gender deficiency.

In many families and entire societies, women are led to feel inferior or inadequate due to their biological nature and gender-assigned roles. These are all ways of transmitting shame from one generation to another.

Freedom from this kind of shame requires intervention into the systemic nature of shame. If there is some forgotten secret, the discovery of the secret does not produce freedom from shame. It may only reinforce it. This means that the cause of shame is of less importance in recovery than the pattern of shame. Only when the pattern of abuse is broken and the self begins the process of recovery is there an end to this kind of shame abuse.

The self-abuse in a shame-based system is difficult to discover and deal with because the system operates in what appears to be a normal and structured way. Bradshaw reminds us of this when he says: "Shame-based families operate according to the laws of social systems. When a social system is dysfunctional, it is rigid and closed. All the individuals in that family are enmeshed into a kind of trance-like frozenness. They take care of the system's need for balance."[13]

Shame, I have suggested, is a form of self-abuse. This is what makes recovery so difficult. Shame cannot be removed by retaliation against others, nor by punishing an offender. Shame does not always disappear when one is freed from guilt, nor can it be relieved by reassurances that there is no objective reason for these feelings of self-recrimination.

Letting Go of the Shame that Hurts

There is no one hurting more from shame than the one feeling it. The self becomes the primary victim of punishing shame. It is a form of abuse where the self is both the abuser and victim. At the same time, shame spreads its poison through the family system and creates shame-based relationships.

Shame is not overcome through "self-help" techniques alone, although growing out of shame is a process of self-recovery. Professional psychotherapeutic intervention into the abuse of shame is often necessary. Along with therapeutic intervention, however, recovery from the self-abuse of shame requires a resocializing of the self with non–shame-based people.

The splitting of the self into accuser and victim lies behind the power of shame to abuse the self. To stop this abuse, the self must recover its sense of personal worth, unity and belonging in a non–shame-based relationship.

Recovery from the destructive power of shame means letting go of the shame which abuses, while retaining a capacity for shame. The goal is not to become shameless, but to value and esteem the self as not shameful. Three elements of this process are: *Uncovering*, followed by *recovering* and finally *discovering*.[14]

Uncovering the Secret of Shame

Shame thrives on secrecy, and secrecy is its most powerful defense. What shame fears most of all is the uncovering of the self in its wretched and disgusting condition. It is instructive that, in the first recorded instance of shame in the Bible, Adam and Eve covered themselves with fig leaves when they "knew that they were naked" (Genesis 3:7). When God found them hiding in the garden and called out to them, "Where are you?", the man explained, "I heard the sound of you in the garden, and I was afraid, because I was naked; and I hid myself" (3:10). "Who told you that were naked?" replied God.

The relation of nakedness to shame no doubt has more than a literary origin in this text. Nakedness is a metaphor of a self-perception rather than of physical exposure. To "know that one is naked" is a self-perception which causes fear of exposure to arise. Thus the clothing of oneself is a further metaphor of the self's desperate attempt at concealment. This is the beginning of the ritual abuse of shame. Any threat of exposure causes the self to turn against itself and force into hiding what is deemed too ugly to reveal.[15]

Self-recovery begins when a pattern is broken. This may result from an encounter with another person sufficient to stop ritual abusive behavior. Shame isolates and alienates as the self ritualizes self-condemnation, even though one is bound to some social system. Encounter means a breakthrough by which one is arrested in one's tracks, and stopped from continuing an action which is destructive and self-defeating.

"I was pounding away at my son verbally, blaming him for not having the guts to stick to his commitment to the track team," a man once confided to me. "Suddenly, I heard my six-year-old daughter say to me, 'Daddy, you're hurting him!' Thanks to her, I caught myself in time and recovered my perspective. I was supposed to be encouraging him, not punishing him."

The uncovering of shame came as a realization that he was projecting onto his son his own lack of self-worth. The self-condemnation of shame spilled over into a verbal tirade against his son for what he perceived to be a weakness. Shame often leads to the blaming of others as a projection of self-blame.

The father who shared with me his experience of recovery, had begun the first step of recovery. He realized that it was not enough to stop the shaming of his son as a projection of his own self-abuse of shame. He had a lot of uncovering to do in order to continue the work of self-recovery. In our counseling, this work was begun, but soon it had to be extended into other relationships in his life.

I hesitated to encourage him to do recovery work with his own family. The family was much too bound up in shame-based relationships. Instead, I encouraged him to join a support group with whom he could begin the process of uncovering what his shame had forced into hiding. These were feelings of shame that needed to be opened up and shared, not incidents or actions.

With this group he found reinforcement for positive affirmations about himself that did not depend upon keeping his shame feelings secret. At the same time, he recovered the capacity for shame as a positive indicator of the integrity and honesty he had achieved with them. He now could anticipate the shame that would follow from any action by failing to be honest with his feelings. This healthy sense of shame empowered him to maintain the integrity of those relationships and to build a new base for his self-concept as worthy of being known and trusted.

With the uncovering of his shame as a feeling of unworthiness, this man began the journey toward the recovery of a healthy capacity for shame based on his self-worth rather than self-blame.

Recovering the Capacity for Shame

I was "stopped in my tracks" by the traffic officer, and I still feel to this day the burning shame of being made to feel like a little boy caught doing something wrong by his father. I guess that those incidents made me a more cautious driver due to the threat of being caught again. I have learned to use my rear view mirror more consistently when driving with the pack on the freeway. I relish the feeling when I see some other poor sucker get caught and forced to go through what I did. But this is not recovery!

Recovery has to do with catching myself in the act of shaming myself. When that process begins, I am in recovery if I "catch myself in time" and shift from self-condemnation to self-evaluation. "Why am I doing this to myself?" I ask. "Am I not supposed to like myself rather than to hate myself?"

"Why are you hurting yourself?" is the voice that I need to hear. But this voice must come from someone who has the power to intercept the blind and brutal assault on the self by the self. The man who shared with me his own recovery moment admitted that if his wife had said the same thing, he probably would have turned his rage on her as well. The six-year-old girl had access to a vulnerable part of him, but also stood outside the pattern of shame in which he was caught.

Recovery cannot begin until the most vulnerable part of our self-image is opened up with the innocence of a child's question. There was no perceived blame in the child's question, nothing to stir the hidden shame into reaction, or to cause further shame. Rather, the child, by her intervention, actually empowered the father to recover his own sense of shame at what he was doing.

Recovery is about having a capacity for shame without feeling shamed. This is almost impossible to do when shame has already produced self-imposed alienation and isolation. The capacity for shame has become distorted and twisted into an instrument to be used in the ritual abuse of self-shaming.

Recovery begins with an intervention into this self-abusive dynamic. I believe that it can only happen when someone or something touches the most vulnerable part of us with sufficient innocence to cause us to recover, for a moment at least, a capacity for shame. The painful, but accurate insight that one suffers from shame as a form of self-abuse, must be linked to the assumption that one has the power to do good because one is actually good. This involves recovering the capacity for shame as a positive and healthy core of the self.

Recovery can only follow from uncovering the shame which binds the self and blinds it to its own essential worth. Once the penetration has been made into the vulnerable core of the self and the self has recovered, "just in time," from its programmed ritual of self-abuse, the process of recovery can continue.

Recovering a capacity for shame based on a positive valuing of the self results from the affirmation of a non–shame-based network of relationships. Uncovering the secret of hidden shame is the first step. Recovering a capacity for healthy shame through the renewal of self-worth is the second. "Only a very noble being can feel shame," Smedes reminds us.

Recovering a sense of nobility is a humbling and yet empowering discovery. The recovery of self-worth, says Smedes, is what the grace of God does when it heals our shame. "A grace that makes us feel worse for having it is an ungracious grace and therefore not really grace at all. If grace heals our shame, it must be a grace that tells us we are worthy to have it. We need, I believe, to recognize that we are accepted not only in spite of our undeserving but because of our worth."[16]

Discovering the Blessing of Freedom from Shame

The goal of recovery is discovery. This is the awakening to the reality of self-recovery similar to the experience of breaking through to the crest of a hill after a steep climb and seeing the expanded horizon of new vistas opened up to one's gaze. New possibilities emerge out of the discovery that the self is anchored in place by a positive unity of perception and affirmation.

On occasion, in the process of pastoral counseling, I have had a person come in for an appointment after many weeks of struggle and exclaim: "I don't know what has happened. But I awakened this morning and the feeling that I had a weight tied around my neck was gone! I feel free from the burden that we have been trying to get rid of and full of hope and expectation such as I have not had for years."

To tell the truth, I was as surprised as the person who experienced it! It was not as though I concluded the session a week prior with the knowledge that next week would produce the breakthrough. It was only in retrospect that I could look back and see the signs of recovery which had led to the discovery of a newfound sense of peace and wholeness. Discovery has to do with the realization that a transformation has taken place deep within the self.[17]

The biblical concept of blessing was surely meant to empower the self with a sense of worth and value. Shame produces what some psychologists have called a "narcissistic injury" to the self. The self-love which is a God-created image in the human self through which we seek fulfillment and pleasure, is wounded and crippled by shame. In our desperate search for happiness we seek rights and benefits when what we really need is blessing.

The feeling of being blessed can only be described, it cannot be defined. It is something that one must experience. It cannot be taught but it can be learned. There is no technique by which it can be achieved, but there is a pathway that leads toward it—it is more of a discovery than a discipline.[18]

When the apostle Paul contemplated his life through the lens of acceptance in Jesus Christ, he saw that his recovery began when he was intercepted on the Damascus road by the Spirit of Jesus Christ. Having been "stopped in his tracks" by this encounter, he heard the voice of Jesus ask him why he was hurting himself. "Saul, Saul, why are you persecuting me? It hurts you to kick against the goads" (Acts 26:14). Thus began his recovery followed by his uncovery. " . . . I was formerly a blasphemer, a persecutor, and a man of violence. But I received mercy. . . . " (1 Tim. 1:13).

Paul was well aware of the terrible consequences of attempting to fulfill his own need for righteousness. He confessed that he became a "wretched man," captive to his desperate desires so that the "law of sin" was working within him. Yet, in the midst of this confession he cries out, " . . . I delight in the law of God in my inmost self" (Rom. 7:22). At the very core of his being, Paul does not deny or devalue himself. He feels that God has loved him and called him to be a child of God. "We boast in our hope of sharing the glory of God," Paul wrote, and "hope does not disappoint us, because God's love has been poured into our hearts through the Holy Spirit that has been given to us" (Rom. 5:2,5).

When Jacob fled from his brother Esau, after conspiring to rob him of his birthright, he was in state of turmoil and uncertainty. He had acquired the birthright but had not gained the blessing of inner peace. What appeared to be flight from the only place that he had known and the only family that he had, dysfunctional as it was, turned out to be a pilgrimage to promise. Falling asleep in the wilderness, with a stone for a pillow, he dreamed of angels ascending and descending on a ladder that reached into Heaven.

Awakening, he cried out: "Surely the Lord is in this place—and I did not know it!" (Gen. 28:16). The hard stone of shame became a ladder of blessing through a vision of God's grace in his life.

Jacob set up the stone as an altar to God, naming the place Bethel—house of God. While this marked the spot where he made the discovery as a religious shrine, the greater significance was the discovery deep within himself that he was really blessed by God. Up to that time he no doubt felt shame at the means used to secure the birthright at the expense of his brother Esau. Whatever the wrong done to that relationship and the guilt incurred, and later he would make recompense for that, it was nothing compared to the shame which he carried away in his soul.

Jacob's discovery was the internalizing of the blessing which now came directly from God's own word. He arrived at the place under the burden of shame, and left with a blessing in his heart. Now he has the blessing, and the shame is gone, and with it its power of self-condemnation.

There is a blessing for us, that the hard stone of crushing shame and self-condemnation can be turned into a ladder with angels carrying manna from Heaven to feed our starved souls! It is wise for us as well to have an outward point of reference for the inner experience of blessing. Bethel marks the place of discovery and the beginning of recovery. There is freedom to continue the journey knowing that the blessing is abiding in our hearts and the stone remains to mark the place.[19]

CHAPTER TWELVE

Recovering from Broken Promises and Personal Grief

My joy is gone, grief is upon me, my heart is sick (Jeremiah 8:18). For the Lord will not reject forever. Although he causes grief, he will have compassion according to the abundance of his steadfast love; for he does not willingly afflict or grieve anyone. (Lamentations 3:31-33)

"But daddy, you promised!" I stared back into the eyes of a girl who had learned to trust the face that was always there for her and the arms that had never failed to be open to her. How fragile, I wondered, was her faith? Could she survive the loss of what she had expected, or would a promise which could not be kept today shatter her trust in another tomorrow? Were these pitiful expressions of pain mere surface scratches which could be erased from life's chalkboard or volcanic eruptions issuing from the core of her being?

"It simply isn't possible today, my dear. Someone has

died and I have a funeral to conduct. Next week, for sure, I
will take you to Disneyland. And I tell you what, I will
make it up to you by getting the tricycle you have been
begging for."

It worked, of course. While she had no way of compre-
hending the priority of another person's grief over her own
pleasure, she was quick to trade her present loss for a
promised gift, or so it seemed.

Sooner or later, she will discover that a substitute pleasure for a searing loss is not a fair trade. She will discover
that her grief, not merely her loss, has priority on the balance scales of life. And what will she do then?

The Life Cycle of Loss and Recovery

There is a cycle in life, and we must all pass through the
stages, more than once, it seems. It is a cycle of separation, attachment, loss, and survival. Torn from the fetal
cocoon and separated at birth from the nourishing cord of
common life by the snip of a scissors, the human infant is
set adrift both physically and emotionally on the ocean of
humanity. However tranquil the waters may be in the snug
harbor of the caregiver's calm, the self of the newborn is
sensitized to the stirring of distant storms and trembles.
Seismic tremors of future shocks are already being recorded on the psychic Richter scale of the anxious self. To be
human is to bear the inherent knowledge of ultimate loss as
a threat to one's being.

This natal separation is healed, more or less, by attachment to others who give us names, offer care, and make
promises. The losses come early and give warning of more
to come. The first denial of the mother's breast, the broken
toy which cannot be fixed, the broken promises which
crush the spirit, these confront the child with the scarcity of

grace and the impact of grief. There are new toys to replace the broken ones, another puppy to make up for the one that died, and new and better promises to make one forget the ones not kept.

Most of us survive, only to discover that this was an elementary schooling in life's curriculum of promise and pain. Before we are through, we will have a university degree in survival skills or, be sent back by life to repeat the same course which we did not pass. For some of us, life can get stuck, like the broken cycle of an automatic washing machine, we keep drenching our souls with grief and never get to "spin dry."

Follow me as I tell again the story of our first parents. Here we will discover that what happens to each of us is common to all of us.

The biblical story of human origins replicates the life cycle of the self from its natal alienation and subsequent bonding through a near fatal loss and consequent survival. There is sorrow here, people, feel it! There is joy, too, a clasping of self with self, enhanced by the subliminal loneliness which, like a dream, disappears with the dawning of the day.

"This at last is bone of my bones and flesh of my flesh," cried the man, awakening out of his primordial trance and solitary silence, ". . . and they became one flesh" (Gen. 2:23, 24). The figure of the divine is in the background, slightly offstage, writing the script as the drama unfolds. The author and the actors are part of a piece; in their respective roles, each alike embracing the whole.

"In the day that you eat of it you shall die," comes the whisper from the wings offstage (Gen. 2:17). A word of wisdom if one is prone to be cautious; a shiver of excitement if one is inclined to be curious. But what is this talk about death? In the innocence of spiritual puberty, what could be known about death that it should be a possibility if not an inevitability?

Ah, the storyteller reminds us, we always know more than we can tell. There is a knowledge at the core of the self for which we will never find words. It rises up within us without our bidding and cannot be forgotten or erased by the most strenuous act of the will nor by the most delirious ecstasy of emotion.

In the bond of love and attachment experienced by the first man and woman, each has a knowledge of the absence of the other. In the pleasure of life's most gratifying moments, there is a knowledge of the passing away of that life, and that is death. In the most self-assured managing of one's possessions in life, there is the knowledge of their impending loss.

Anne Morrow Lindberg, who once gazed into the face of her perfect infant son, only to have him snatched by a kidnapper into oblivion, saw too that perfection carries within it the seeds of fragmentation and loss.

> Within the hollow wave there lies a world,
> Gleaming glass-perfect, rising to be hurled
> Into a thousand fragments on the sand,
> Driven by tide's inexorable hand.
> Now in the instant while disaster towers,
> I glimpse a land more beautiful than ours;
> Another sky, more lapis-lazuli,
> Lit by unsetting suns; another sea
> By no horizon bound; another shore,
> Glistening with shells I never saw before.
> Smooth mirror of the present, poised between
> The crest's "becoming" and the foams "has been"—
> How luminous the landscape seen across
> The crystal lens of an impending loss![1]

For Adam and Eve, when the forbidden fruit was eaten, the consequence came as no surprise, though the pain of the loss was incomprehensible. "Cursed is the ground because of you; in toil you shall eat it all the days of your life. . . . By the sweat of your face you shall eat bread until you return to the ground, for out of it you were taken; you are dust, and to dust you shall return. . . . therefore the Lord God sent him forth from the garden of Eden . . ." (Gen. 3:17-23). "Now the man knew his wife, Eve, and she conceived and bore Cain, saying, 'I have produced a man with the help of the Lord'" (Gen. 4:1).

Yes, they survived, even this tragic loss. And so the cycle is complete. Human life does not begin in a vacuum; the self does not emerge without shadows of the darkness to which it is prone. Bonding to another satisfies the deepest longing of the self for connection but creates its own pain of separation and loss. Love intensifies the suffering when love is lost.

"Yet no one loves another without becoming vulnerable to the other, without being affected by the other, and, if need be, suffering with the other; hence one who loves, especially with a steadfast love, will necessarily be changed in the loving relationship."[2]

We can no more split the joy of love apart from the pain of loss than we can cut the story of our origins out of the narrative of our life. There was no age of innocence without a knowledge of death and no joining of the self with another without the "not good" of being alone and disconnected.

The first shock of experiencing a loss is that of betrayal. When we lose that which we hold dear and that upon which we have placed our hope and trust, the whiplash of betrayal leaves an unhealed slash on the most tender spot of the self.

Why Betrayal Hurts So Much

I saw it in a men's restroom in a restaurant in San Francisco. It was printed in block letters with a blue felt pen across the top of the mirror: JUDAS COME HOME, ALL IS FORGIVEN. The name of Judas, who betrayed Jesus with a kiss, has become a synonym for an act so treacherous and so fatal to the self that recovery seems impossible. Judas, in fact, went out and hung himself. Having betrayed the one who chose him and loved him, Judas could not find the grace to recover from the injury which he had inflicted upon himself.

What struck me so powerfully in reading this graffiti was the possibility of recovery for even one like Judas. What remained with me was the thought that there is a bit of Judas in each of us. As much as we want to find a Judas to become the scapegoat for the intrusion of evil into the good, we cannot pretend our own innocence.

The power to hurt comes with the capacity to love. Only those who dare to love have the power to destroy that love through betrayal. Betrayal is a secret which every promise pretends not to see.[3]

We do not expect to be reminded of betrayal at the exchange of wedding vows. The illusion of "perfect love" is like a wedding garment cast over the naked reality of imperfect lovers. These are injured selves making promises not to hurt. These are selves capable of deadly violence making vows to promote safety and serenity. These are persons who do not fully trust themselves entrusting their happiness to one another.

We inoculate children against the most deadly childhood diseases, while entrusting them to parents whose best intentions carry the virus of violence and abuse. We bless the children with sacramental grace as a sign of divine favor and, in some cases, with the hope of the implantation of a spiritual nature. Yet, experience teaches us that they are born with selves which carry the seeds of hatred as well as of love, and a capacity for self-inflicted injury that is not washed away in the baptismal font.

While we suffer much from the actions and failures of others, we inflict the most grievous injury upon ourselves. Why is it that we can begin life with such idealism and optimism and end by losing or destroying the very things we cherish the most?

With the death of a loved one there may be anger, self-pity, regret, and even feelings of blame and self-accusation. "If only . . ." "Why didn't I . . . ?" The death of love, however, has its own kind of grief. With the breaking of a promise, there is a sense of failure and betrayal that cuts both ways. We can never be absolutely certain that we are not the ones who have failed. There was only one betrayer of Jesus, but each of the disciples shuddered with the possibility that he was the one! "They began to be distressed and to say to him one after another, 'Surely, not I?'" (Mark 14:19). When love has died and promises have been broken, each one is an accomplice of the betrayal of a vow.

Betrayal is like a fault in an otherwise perfect diamond. It is not a scratch on the surface that can be rubbed out. Hurts can heal, sometimes with only the faintest scar. But when a fault occurs, like betrayal, what was once a jewel can look like junk. This is what makes recovery so difficult. In our despair, we are tempted to trash our treasures.

The Anatomy of Betrayal

The reality of love grows where the intentions of the heart are focused and shared. Attachments are also forms of commitments and we are bound to one another through shared promises and expressed love. But in that love are also found the source of betrayal and the seeds of treachery. We can do injury to a stranger, but this is not betrayal. If a manufacturer fails to honor a warranty on a product, I am angry at the injustice but it is not betrayal. A robber may break into my house and steal my property and violate my space. I am outraged but I do not feel betrayed. It is easier to forget a crime than to forgive a friend.

When the attachments which offer the self an orientation in the world give way and break apart, the self experiences more than the natal separation anxiety. The loss of the attachments which have enabled the self to form a self-identity in relationship to others threatens the very core of the self. It is one thing to feel an existential sense of aloneness and separation. It is quite another to mourn the death of a loved one, the loss of a relationship, or the betrayal of trust. A broken promise cuts deeper into the self than unfulfilled desire. I can weep for something which may never come to pass, but my heart is broken when the love which came to pass is taken from me. We may survive such losses but never fully recover the capacity to love and trust again.

The Psalmist seems to be writing out of painful personal experience when he writes: "Even my bosom friend in whom I trusted, who ate of my bread, has lifted the heel against me" (Psalm 41:9). "It is not enemies who taunt me—I could bear that; it is not adversaries who deal insolently with me—I could hide from them. But it is you, my equal, my companion, my familiar friend, with whom I kept pleasant company; . . . " (Psalm 55: 12-14).

The very concept of betrayal requires that there be something to betray. And in betrayal it is love that is both the source and the object. We betray when we feel that our own love is betrayed by the failure of others. We become treacherous when we test the vision of love and find it different than our own. When we feel betrayed, we turn the passion of love into raging violence and ruthless vengeance when that which we love seems to fail our expectations and resist our demands.

How else do we explain the fact that domestic violence and child abuse is treachery against the people that we have promised to love? What could account for the fact that "normal" people abuse and seek to destroy those with whom they live other than the fact that before there was betrayal, there was love? Only when trust is first formed through shared life can it be broken. And only the sense of outrage, fueled by a primitive moral instinct, and carried out with the passion of love's despair can wreak the havoc and destruction in a family and among friends that betrayal causes.

At the core of the psyche of the betrayer is failed love, not an evil spirit. Betrayers need more than forgiveness which issues from the love of another. Both the betrayer and the betrayed need the recovery of a love within themselves that has gone awry. This is why it is so difficult for those who have betrayed others to be received back into fellowship through repentance and forgiveness. For betrayal has torn the flesh of fellowship and friendship away, leaving only the skeleton of love's despair visible. This is too terrible to look upon and too revealing of the fear that hides in our own love, for us to tolerate.

Why Survivors Find it Hard to Make Promises

When Jerry and Paula (not their real names) asked me to work with them in preparing for their marriage, they made it clear that this was a second marriage for both of them. Each had gone through the painful process of a failed first marriage and worked through the grief process. They were survivors, they told me, and were now ready to make a commitment to each other in hopes that this time they could be more realistic.

As I read over the marriage vows, and came to the phrase, "so long as we both shall live," Jerry interrupted me and said. "I cannot say that. I failed in my first vow and do not feel that in all honesty I can make such an unconditional promise again. It is not fair to Paula." As we discussed the implication of what was being said, he suggested an alternative reading: "As long as we both shall love." In his mind, this conditional vow of love had more integrity than an unconditional one. He was attempting to be realistic, acknowledging the fact that love can die. Paula was disturbed by the conditional character of his suggestion, and was quite willing to have the original form of the vow used.

I argued in return, that the very nature of love is unconditional and that trust in each other was grounded in a commitment that reached beyond the failures of the past. In any event, he allowed me to proceed in accordance with the original vows, though he personally held to his reservations. As it turned out, after no more than three years, the marriage has apparently come to an end. Paula left the relationship over problems in the marriage which Jerry acknowledges to be largely his fault. He continues to insist that he loves her while she says that love has died.

What Jerry never really grasped, apparently, was that "as long as we both shall love" really was a condition which left *him* an escape clause in the marriage, but not her! The shock of the failed marriage is a blow to him. His pain and grief are deep and devastating. The fact that she no longer loves him does not diminish for a moment the sense of loss he feels.

Each in their own way, are now thrown back into the cycle where attachment has led to loss, and where the process of grieving moves toward survival. Jerry considered himself to be a survivor and sought to protect himself from further pain by qualifying his commitment and making his promise conditional on love. His assumption was that if love dies then there would be no loss, or at least, the loss would be less devastating and destructive. But it doesn't work that way! The death of love is always an unqualified loss. The breaking of a promise is a tear in the fabric of the self that goes to the core.

Can recovery take place when the losses of life are so pervasive, so permanent, and so painful? The answer is yes; but the key is finding the place to begin and the resources to help.

Grieving through to Grace

It is the self which has been wounded in every loss, whether through the death of a loved one, the death of love, or the searing pain of betrayal. All losses need to be grieved, no matter how trivial they may seem to others. Each person's loss is greater than that of others. For losses are personally weighted not progressively graded. It is the experience of divine grace, often mediated through the care and love others, that finally enables us to recover from loss. Grief is the process of reaching that grace.

Grief has to do with feelings, and feelings are the self, as I suggested in the first chapter of this book. Self-recovery begins with finding those feelings which lead directly to the core of the self. The self is formed through a cycle of separation, attachment, loss, and survival. This means that the core of the self must always be prepared to integrate separation into attachment and loss into survival. Most people survive out of necessity as much as out of grace.

In the cycle of self-development, attachment carries implicit commitment and the promise always to be there when needed. In this bond is the premonition of a future loss. In many cases this loss does not occur through the death of a loved one, but through a succession of broken promises and finally the death of love.

The self is capable of its own survival in an amazing way under normal circumstances. In the same way, the physical body is capable of healing itself—a miraculous thing when we think about it! The goal is to get back on your feet and run the race, even if you can no longer finish first. Physicians, physical therapists and psychotherapists count on this phenomenon more than on their technical skills!

When recovery has survival as its main goal, however, it is like getting back on a horse immediately after having been thrown off. The thing to overcome is the fear of horses, even if we have not increased our skill in riding!

I suspect that the reason a higher percentage of marriages fail the second time around is related to the same phenomenon. A second marriage can be an attempt to prove to oneself that one is not afraid of marriage, even though one has not recovered the skills necessary to form a lasting relationship. Surviving loss is not the same as recovering the creative life of the self.

When the self is hurting, the felt need is reduction of pain. Therapists tell me that the single most inhibiting factor in self-recovery is the need to feel better rather than to follow the pain back to the core of the self. Clients want their therapists to reduce pain, not to probe the hurt.

When we are caught in the throes of grieving a loss, it is sometimes hard to grow out of the grief. The intense feeling of grief can sometime be the only way to remain connected to what has been lost. When this happens we get stuck in the loss cycle of recovery, unable to move on to survival. Grief becomes a ritual of attachment to what no longer exists, hindering our growth toward the grace of recovery.

Just the opposite can happen as well. The feeling of grief can be so great that it becomes repressed and a "will to survive" takes over. "I'm a survivor," these persons like to say, as if to assure themselves that, while they have suffered loss, the game of life is not over.

There is a kind of self-therapy that works the same way. The coping mechanisms that enable the self to survive the onslaught of anxiety, pain, and grief provide the skeletal structure for survival. Around this structure, denial and suppression of feelings build layers of psychic muscle which reinforces the will to survive. What forces one to get back on the horse, despite the paralyzing fear, is the need to overpower the shame and regain recognition among one's peers. This is survival, not recovery. The psychic energy it takes to maintain the defenses against anxiety and emotional pain for the sake of survival depletes the self of its resources for recovery.

Grieving through to grace goes beyond survival to the recovery of the self's capacity to love without fear and to be loved without shame. Grace is growth and growth moves through phases, each adding strength to hope and faith. Grace empowers the self, enabling it to retain the memory of what was lost while letting go of the object that was lost.

Grace comes from outside the self as empowering love and resides within the self as the "courage to be."[4] The will to survive may express defiance in the face of a loss. "Courage to be" expresses acceptance of the loss through an expansion of the horizons of the self. Survival narrows life to the single task of defeating the enemy. Grace

expands life by stitching a loss into the mosaic of the pat-
terned quilt which we are creating to bequeath to those
who follow us.

Because grace is creative it has its source in a Creator
God. Because grace is restorative it has its power in a
Redeemer God. Because grace is inspiring it communi-
cates its life through the Spirit of God. Through grief we
apprehend the grace of God, and by the grace of God we
recover the courage to be.

Walk with me through the passageway from grief to
grace and discover recovery.

The Phases of Recovery

Recovery moves in phases, not in progressive steps.
Recovery is not like climbing a ladder or drawing by the
numbers. I have high regard for the numerous variations of
the twelve-step programs for recovery. But my own view
is that recovery is more like moving through phases of
growth than progressing through stages of behavior modifi-
cation.

What makes the twelve-step concept work, in my judgment, is not the steps alone, but (1) the unqualified abandonment of self-therapy, including an intolerance for self-
deception, (2) the unconditional acceptance by others,
including a structure of accountability, and (3) an expanding self-horizon, including the courage to be. There is
often a spiritual component in these programs, not as a
clearly defined doctrine of God, but as an assurance that
there is a capacity for renewal and hope within the self that
can directly tap the resource of a divine, higher power.

A physical therapist will require that a patient exercise
the muscles in order to facilitate the phases of recovery
through the body's own resources for wholeness.

Manipulation of body parts does not heal, it only forces the body to function in a way that promotes health. Recovery, in this sense, is a process of going through the phases of growth which lead to the restoration of life at its optimum possibility, given whatever limits and restrictions still apply.

1. The abandonment of self-therapy

The dark shadows of a critical loss of love and trust cause us to move toward the light in hopes of ridding our lives of pain and healing the sickness of grief. Self-therapy includes all of our attempts to overcome pain, conceal the hurt, and clothe the self with new images of purposeful and productive life. The critical point in recovery occurs when all such attempts are abandoned and one's life is exposed to a greater healing power.

The power of self-deception is what makes self-therapy appear to work. When self-deception is exposed and no longer tolerated, the self is stripped of its most effective defense against the truth and prepared to see what had been hidden by the false light of self-therapy.

In the biblical story of the healing of a man blind from birth, a sub-plot emerges in the controversy which ensues between Jesus and the religious authorities who opposed Him (John 9). They denied at first that the man was really blind and that a healing had occurred. The man himself was not deceived. "One thing I do know, that though I was blind, now I see." In refusing to believe the man's story, they themselves, as it were, had become blind. "If you were blind, you would not have sin. But now that you say, 'We see,' your sin remains" (John 9:41). Their "sin" was the blindness of self-deception and failure to recognize the grace of God which brought healing and hope to the blind man.

There are phases of recovery in which darkness enters

again so that the cycle of the self may be fully integrated in its growth toward wholeness and health.

The moon is not always luminous and full, nor does it become permanently stuck in a phase with only a sliver of its self showing. Perhaps this is why primitive people were more attuned to the phases of the moon than the rising and setting of the sun. The sun has no phases. It is either burning so bright that one cannot bear to look directly at it, obscured from view by clouds, or gone completely in the "dead of night." The moon, as we all know, not only passes through its phases corresponding to the cycle of the self, but it is our companion in the night.

In his play, *After the Fall,* Arthur Miller provided a brilliant analysis of the journey to self-recovery in the form of the lead character, Quentin. After failed marriages and the betrayal of his commitment to love Maggie, Quentin speaks:

> You ever felt you once saw yourself—absolutely true? I may have dreamed it, but I swear that somewhere along the line—with Maggie, I think—for one split second I saw my life; what I had done, what had been done to me, and even what I ought to do. And that vision sometimes hangs behind my head, blind now, bleached out like the moon in the morning; and if I could only let in some necessary darkness it would shine again. I think it had to do with power.[5]

My father used to plant potatoes every spring. First we would cut them into pieces, making sure that each piece had an "eye" in it, as he called it. From this "eye" a sprout would form and then the pieces were ready to be placed in the ground. One thing remained, however, before we could plant. To ensure a good harvest of potatoes, my father said, we must plant them when the moon is full. So we would wait until the propitious moment, and then place them in the ground.

Come fall, we always had sufficient potatoes, as I recall. In those days, I did not venture to submit this folk wisdom to a scientific test by deliberately planting some during another phase of the moon. I doubt that he did either. It was probably the only superstition that I recall my father ever including in his otherwise common sense approach to the tilling of the soil and the husbandry of our livestock.

Even as I write this, why do I feel a sense of uneasiness in making such a clear distinction between superstition and common sense? He would not have been happy with such a charge. For him, the working of the soil was a participation in a cycle of sowing and reaping, suffering crop failures and rejoicing at bountiful harvests. He never disclosed his inner feelings, neither of grief at his losses nor joy at his successes. I gather now that he lived a self-life in communion with the seasons of nature, with the rhythm of birth, life and death and, yes, by the phases of the moon! This may be the most common of all senses!

2. Unconditional acceptance by others

A second phase of recovery from the grief of loss moves us into relationships which offer unconditional acceptance. Actually, this phase overlaps with the first, for without this offer of unconditional acceptance, the abandonment of self-therapy cannot move forward to grace. Grace, as I have suggested, comes from outside the self as empowering love. Only love which is experienced as unconditional acceptance empowers the self.

Self-acceptance is always conditional because it is qualified by feelings of unworthiness and knowledge of our own failures. If self-acceptance becomes unconditional then it is based on self-deception. It is only the experience of being loved and accepted by someone else without qualification and with no strings attached, that frees us from self-deception and, at the same time, empowers us to love and accept ourselves.

Unconditional love does not reward our strengths and punish our weaknesses. Unconditional acceptance does not say, "You are important to me and I care for you, but you must get over this loss and get on with life." No, unconditional acceptance says, "Because I am committed to you, I will share your grief and feel with you the pain of your loss."

We cannot grieve through to grace without the experience of unconditional love and acceptance, for grace *is* unconditional in giving the gift of love.

It has often been said, "We must love the sinner but hate the sin." I wonder if people who say that have any idea of how destructive and downright ungracious that concept is! Whatever my sins and failures may be, that is who I am! You cannot love me without accepting the whole of me, painful and threatening as that may be.

Love is not a virtue that must be protected by abstractions from the concrete reality of the unlovely. Grief is not a beautiful thing to behold in another and the anger and despair it creates is not conducive to growth in grace by itself. It takes unconditional grace expressed through others being there for us to find and feel the acceptance we need. Blessed are those whose moon passes into this phase!

When others make unconditional commitments to accept us as we are, no strings attached, a structure of accountability is also created through which we can measure our growth. The counter side to "I will be there for you" is, "you will always have me to certify your growth." Accountability is corrective and creative. Accountability is what keeps us from slipping back into self-deception. It is the means of our recovery and the measure of our growth.

Through unconditional acceptance by others, we are drawn out of the narrowness of grief confinement into the spaciousness of grace completeness. The third phase of recovery begins when we begin to think about seeds to sow in the freshly dug soil of self-acceptance.

3. An expanding self-horizon

Self-recovery includes an expansion of the self, allowing time for the fragments of the self to "grow their own eyes" and then find a place in the nourishing soil of the human family. Self-recovery begins with the discovery that what appeared to be a gaping hole in the seamless robe of our fragile happiness is the edge of darkness caused by the setting of the sun. There is no grief that does not have its home in the capacity of the self to suffer loss and still be the self. Grief does not have to kill in order to be grief.

Awakening in the midst of the "dead of night," where the soul lies still and the heart beats softly, there is the rising of the moon, now in the luminous phase of fullness. At last comes the time for sowing, even a second or third time, as Anne Morrow Lindberg poetically puts it, after losing her own son in a tragic kidnapping.

> For whom
> The milk ungiven in the breast
> When the child is gone?

> For whom
> The love locked up in the heart
> That is left alone?

That golden yield
Split sod once, overflowed an August field,
Threshed out in pain upon September's floor,
Now hoarded high in barns, a sterile store.

Break down the door;
Rip open, spread and pour
The grain upon the barren ground
Wherever crack in clod is found.

There is no harvest for the heart alone;
The seed of love must be
Eternally Resown.[6]

Grieving through to grace opens up the vault where grief stores its treasures and ritually mourns its losses. When the golden grain we have harvested, sometimes prematurely, from the first sowing of love becomes new seed for sowing, we are in recovery.

We sow seeds by making promises, making friends, making commitments, and giving the gift of ourself as a living plant to grow in another's garden.

The seeds which we now sow are those which we have reaped from the sorrow and tragedy of earlier losses. This is what the cycle of life teaches us. Watch for your moon, move with its phases, and trust the mystery of life as holding the promise of God.

CHAPTER THIRTEEN

Recovering from Tragic Loss and a Crisis of Faith

My anguish, my anguish! I writhe in pain! Oh, the walls
of my heart! My heart is beating wildly; I cannot keep
silent; for I hear the sound of the trumpet, the alarm of
war. (Jeremiah 4:19)

Sooner or later, each one of us will utter in our own way,
the cry of Jesus from the cross: "My God, my God, why
have you forsaken me?" (Matt. 27:46). "Why, God?" "Why
me, God?" "How could you let this happen, God?" These
are some of the questions I have heard over and over again
in pastoral ministry to persons caught in personal tragedy.

Where is God When Tragedy Strikes?

Some years ago I was asked to make a pastoral call to
counsel a woman who was dying of cancer. She was a
young mother in her middle thirties, with three small children. Her husband was in denial of her illness; he would
not discuss it with her and even avoided coming into her

bedroom where she lay, too weak to get up. As we talked she raged in anger over the fact that God was allowing this to happen to her. "How can God let me die with these small children to care for," she demanded. "I have prayed, but my prayers go unanswered. Why has God abandoned me?"

I attempted to enter into her feelings of anger and agreed that what happened to her was a terrible injustice and a great tragedy. I asked if she was afraid to die, and she replied, "Yes, because I don't know who will take care of my kids, and I have lost my faith in God." Then, looking directly at me, she demanded again, "Tell me, pastor, how do you explain God's absence and His failure to heal me and prevent this terrible thing from happening?"

I felt my formal theological training melt away like a sand castle washed with a cresting wave. To give a defense of God at that moment was beyond my competence. The enormity of the reality of her situation exposed my carefully prepared "textbook" responses as superficial and inane. Venturing into unexplored territory, led only by the flickering light of her own desperate honesty, I replied: "I don't think that God can do anything about it. I think that He feels as helpless and perhaps as angry as you do."

"You can't say that," she protested. "Don't we believe that God is in control and has the power to do anything He wants?" She had been instructed as to what one should believe about God, as it turned out. She knew what one was expected to say about God, but had little idea of what God had to say about her.

"The God that I know was present when His own child was suffering and dying on the cross," I replied. "He was powerless to intervene and remove Him from the cross, for His love is His power, and it took a powerful love to enter into sickness and death in order to provide a way through it for us."

I went on to talk about the reality of God as present in the pain and suffering of His Son, Jesus Christ. I suggested that our concept of power as absolute control over everything from outside was really very superficial and empty of real meaning. She was quiet for a long time. Then she said, quietly and with deep feeling, "I can believe that. I just had to have some point of contact. I couldn't reach Him when I thought of Him being powerful and distant. But I can trust Him if He is willing to die with me."

After a prayer with shared tears, I asked her, "Are you afraid?" And she replied, "Not so much now. When I think of God's love as His power to go through this with me, I don't feel so alone."

As I later reflected upon what had happened in that room, permeated with pain and shadowed by suffering, I realized that a concept of a God who is viewed as omnipotent and all powerful places him outside our perceptions of reality and beyond the reach of our powerless faith. Instead of destroying her faith in God by suggesting that God was not the all-powerful figure she had in her mind, God was made more real to her and, in a paradoxical kind of way, more powerful in relationship to her own suffering than she had ever experienced before.

What she came to realize is that the power of God is not an abstract kind of power as control over everything, but a power of personal presence even in a time of suffering and dying.

The Crisis of Faith in Suffering

Ultimately, the questions which arise out of injury to the self through failure, loss, and abuse become religious questions. For those with religious convictions, the experience of suffering devastating and tragic losses in life, and the pervading presence of evil, can produce a crisis of faith. In the struggle to find meaning and purpose in life, God is the one we hold to be finally accountable.

The depth of human pain is nearly always perceived in contrast to the height of human aspiration. Yet the apostle Paul found that God's truth incorporates both as a paradox.

God's power is made manifest in weakness, wrote Paul, following his own experience of unanswered prayer with regard to his "thorn in the flesh." This is the power of Christ who has Himself entered into the domain of suffering and evil and has overcome that power with the greater power of divine love and restoration to life (2 Cor. 12:8-9).

The starting point for faith in God, as the Hebrew people came to understand, was in their experience of a God who shared their own suffering.[1]

"Only the suffering God can help," wrote Dietrich Bonhoeffer, when he experienced the collapse of the good when confronted by the evil of Hitler's program of destruction.

> The God who is with us is the God who forsakes us (Mark 15:34). The God who lets us live in the world without the working hypothesis of God is the God before whom we stand continually. Before God and with God we live without God. God lets himself be pushed out of the world on to the cross. . . . Here is the decisive difference between Christianity and all religions. Man's religiosity makes him look in his distress to the power of God in the world: God is the *deus ex machina*. The Bible directs man to God's powerlessness and suffering; only the suffering God can help.[2]

When I looked again at the standard theological textbooks, I saw that they had missed this essential starting point for coming to grips with the reality of suffering and the reality of God. When theology begins by defining God as a being located outside of the world, it is impossible to speak of God as participating in the reality of the world without diminishing God's transcendence over the world. When supernatural power is taught as the primary attribute of God, those who become powerless in the face of suffering and evil find it difficult to believe in the existence of God.

Faith in a God who intervenes on behalf of those who are suffering can turn to unbelief when the "righteous" suffer. We who are adults often try to find reasons why our suffering may be deserved. Few of us would claim to be so righteous as to merit God's intervention in every case. But when children suffer and die, our faith is tested to the utmost.

What Kind of God Lets Children Die?

Rabbi Harold Kushner struck a responsive chord in the hearts of many people with his best-selling book, *When Bad Things Happen to Good People*. His son died at the age of 14, following extended illness due to progeria, the "rapid aging disease." As he attempted to answer the question for himself, as to why God would permit such a tragedy if he had the power to prevent it, he arrived at the following conclusion:

> I believe in God. But I do not believe the same things about Him that I did years ago, when I was growing up or when I was a theological student. I recognize His limitations. He is limited in what He can do by laws of nature and by the evolution of human nature and moral freedom. I no longer hold God responsible for illnesses, accidents, and natural disasters, because I realize that I gain little and I lose so much when I blame God for

those things. I can worship a God who hates suffering
but cannot eliminate it, more easily than I can worship a
God who chooses to make children suffer and die, for
whatever exalted reason.[3]

When I ask my students to read this book and respond to
Kushner, a great deal of anxiety is produced. Most feel
sympathetic toward the Rabbi but rush to defend God's
sovereignty. The notion that God is not in absolute control
over every event makes them nervous and fearful that the
power of God is not given due regard.

Invariably, they end by some kind of appeal to God's
permissive will during the interim time, where suffering
continues due to sin, but for which there will be compensation in the end. A concept of God's power is preserved by
appealing to a divine hidden purpose by which greater
good will come out of present evil. I often urge them never
to offer this bit of wisdom to someone who is actually suffering!

Whatever our concept of suffering and the reality of evil,
we do well to remember that for the one who suffers, it will
always be perceived as evil and not as good. Paul Schilling
reminds us: "It is not easy to distinguish between real and
apparent goods and evils, though we dare never forget that
events perceived as evil by the one experiencing them must
be treated seriously because they are evil for him."[4]

To tell a woman that the death of her young child was
God's plan to develop in her a deeper spiritual life and a
stronger character will likely provoke the response. "I
would rather have my child and remain weaker in character, if I had the choice." Some who have gone through the
cycle of self-development, experiencing grief and loss and
who finally survive, may well testify to a faith and hope
that is stronger by virtue of having stood the test. But only

they have the right to make such a statement, and only for themselves.

As one such person said, "Yes, I am a survivor, but someday God is going to have a lot to answer for!"

Can We Trust God's Goodness When Tragedy Strikes?

In the Bible, the story of Job is told in such a way that the Devil is permitted to inflict Job with catastrophic losses, and yet is limited by God as to the destruction of Job himself. God is the author of the drama of life, and He can allow the characters He has placed in the story to run the course of their role and live out the character assigned to each. At the same time, God has the "script under control," so to speak. And this, in the end, is the message of the book of Job.

We are troubled by the fact that the Devil and God seem to conspire against Job, and that God would allow such evil to exist. We want a different story, where we can sort out the good and the bad from the beginning and ensure that we are always on the good side. But we are not the author!

For the Hebrew people, it was sufficient to know that God was not only one who could enter into the drama at will, but who also had the script under control. They knew that salvation was not in a perfected world, but in God who kept the story under control and who could be trusted to preserve their lives in the end.

For Christians, Jesus Christ is not only a human person caught up in the same suffering that befalls all humans. He is the actual presence and reality of God taking upon Himself the evil, pain, and suffering that alienates and isolates humans from each other and from the life of God.

Jesus Christ entered the human drama as the one who

experienced for Himself the power and destruction of evil. At the same time, He was the bearer of God's grace and hope for all who suffer. God's providence is expressed through the power and presence of the Kingdom of God in which evil is understood to be part of the totality of the life which God created, and for which He gives Himself as redeemer. While God did not create evil, He assumes responsibility for it as part of His created world.

Can We Hold God Responsible for Evil?

God does not duck and dodge the reality of evil, attributing it to human sin and blaming it on the Devil. God is the author of the drama, in which pain and pleasure, suffering and joy, good and evil are part of the plot.

Faith means that we as human participants in that drama have the revelation of God himself. He is the author who encompasses the beginning and the end and is Himself participating in the drama even as we live it out. God takes full responsibility. This, at least, is a start.

The Question of Evil and God's Providence

One question we often ask with regard to suffering is: What does it mean to say that God takes responsibility for evil and that we can have faith in Him to do this? The biblical tradition places the problem of evil within the concept of God's providence. God's providence is expressed through his partnership with human persons in suffering, which is the divine power to be present as an advocate in the context of suffering and for the purpose of redeeming those who suffer.

The providence of God is bound to His promise. This promise is a miracle and mystery of divine love. The promise of God is like that of parents. We promise our children that we will be there for them and will support them through their times of difficulty and even suffering. No parent can promise a life free from pain. In the same way, God's providence is not a guarantee of perfect freedom from suffering but a promise that suffering will not have the power to separate us from His love and ultimate purpose for us.

When suffering occurs, we are led directly to God as the one who must ultimately take responsibility. In His taking responsibility through participation in the dilemma of evil, God comes to us in the context of evil and promises redemption from it.

When a child is struck by a crippling disease, as in the case with Rabbi Kushner, the parent is not looked to as a solution to the problem of evil, but as one who binds oneself to the child through loving presence and care. This is a form of redemption from the power of evil, even though the consequences are not removed in this lifetime. Beyond the providence of parental love, is the love of God which is a covenant of eternal love and care beyond this life.

God's providence is experienced through the event of redemption in which He takes evil upon Himself so as to deliver His creation, once and for all, from the power of evil to separate persons from His covenanted purpose and goal.

The Question of Suffering and God's Power

The practical question with regard to evil is, "How can we mediate God's presence and divine power in the face of evil and with those who suffer?" This cannot be done by defending the power of God as an abstract concept of divine sovereignty. Nor can it be done by limiting God to

the constraints of the finite world and so render Him powerless, albeit, full of sympathy and compassion.

We cannot mediate God's presence and power in the
face of evil by resorting to a concept of divine providence
that ordains suffering for some and blessing for others.
God's providence is seen through the life of Jesus and ultimately in His death on the cross. What appears to be a tri-
umph of evil over good is an event of unspeakable horror
wrapped in the arms of God. The crisis of faith drives us
toward the God who Himself cries out with the anguish of
the "godforsaken." It was from the cross that Jesus took
upon His lips the lament of the ancient Hebrew: "My God,
my God, why have you forsaken me?" (Matt. 27:46; Psalm
22:1). In so doing, Jesus took the depths of human despair
into the very heart of God.

The Question of Grief and the Goodness of God

"If God is good, why does He allow us to experience
such grief and suffering when He could prevent it?" I have
been asked this question over and over again by those who
can hardly bear the pain of grief. Can God's goodness be
experienced even through our grief?

Human sorrow and pain is not itself evil. Our grief is,
after all, human grief, and seeks the comfort and healing of
a divine sorrow. Grief can be so devastating, however, that
it can isolate us from the most well-intentioned human
consolation and create a great chasm which seems to separate us hopelessly from divine presence. Left to itself,
human pain and unrelieved grief conceives unbelief and
gives birth to the despair of atheism.

Evil, by whatever name and in whatever form, seeks out
pain and makes its home in grief. That is its business. The

Devil is a parasite that attaches voracious tentacles upon the vulnerable underside of faith, sucking up the bitter broth of human anguish as the sweetest nectar this side of Hell. Unhealed grief can become the host for this bloodless leech whose power is increased as the threshold of pain is raised to the shrieking point. Human pain devoid of divine presence becomes a sickness of the soul and a fertile womb for the demons of doubt and despair.

Against this sickness, the perfections of divine complacency and the motionless wings of angels have no power.

One thing, and one thing only, will cause the tormenting corruption of evil to flee, and that is divine pathos poured out into the cup of human sorrow. Where the suffering God walks, there are no demons and no darkness. The holiness of this divine grief whispers with the muffled thunder of divine wrath against all that destroys, all that corrupts. The Devil is evil, but cannot suffer and has no compassion. God is good. His goodness is the suffering and compassion demonstrated in bearing human pain to the final limit. Where God is present, there may be suffering, but no evil. Where God is present there may be pain, but no despair.

This can no longer be a godforsaken place. Here is a divine pathos so powerful that pain, by comparison, is weaker, and grief, in contrast, is shallower. Even the demons draw back from the holiness of this divine outpouring of suffering love, and the Devil turns aside as though to gaze upon such beauty would blind the eyes of evil.

Faith reaches for the hand of God, and finds it torn by the nails which bound Christ to the cross. Faith cries out to the heart of God, and finds it bruised and broken by the anguish of betrayal. Faith looks up to the face of God and sees the tears of sorrow for unbearable pain.

Grieving Through to Faith

The process of grieving a loss is paradoxical in its intention. Through grief one seeks to heal the pain of loss, let go of what can no longer be kept, and face the reality of living with only a memory of what once was. At the same time, there is a sense of responsibility not to forget what was lost. "If I forget you, O Jerusalem," the Psalmist cries out. "Let my tongue cling to the roof of my mouth, . . . if I do not set Jerusalem above my highest joy" (Psalm 137:5-6). Can we give ourselves permission to experience a present "highest joy" without betraying a former one?

The paradox in grieving the loss of a loved one is that recovery from the loss can be seen as betrayal of the one who was loved. Our grief becomes our only expression of loyalty, as if to be healed would be to abandon the love that once bound us together.

The Christian author C. S. Lewis, following the death of his wife, wrote in *A Grief Observed* of his intense need to remain in grief for his wife as a way of remaining in contact with her. At first, after her death, to let go of his intense grief was to feel that he was abandoning her.

"We don't really want grief, in its first agonies, to be prolonged; nobody could. But we want something else of which grief is a frequent symptom. . . . we want to live our marriage well and faithfully through that phase too. If it hurts (and it certainly will) we accept the pains as a necessary part of this phase. We don't want to escape them at the price of desertion or divorce. Killing the dead a second time." Through his own painful process, however, Lewis discovered, "passionate grief does not link us with the dead but cuts us off from them."[5]

Grieving through to faith is something like suffering through a dark night of the soul and then experiencing the sudden breaking of a new dawn.

C. S. Lewis, during this process of recovery, reported:

> Something quite unexpected. has happened. It came this morning early. For various reasons, not in themselves at all mysterious, my heart was lighter than it had been for many weeks. For one thing, I suppose I am recovering physically from a good deal of mere exhaustion. And I'd had a very tiring but very healthy twelve hours the day before, and a sounder night's sleep; and after ten days of low-hung grey skies and motionless warm dampness, the sun was shining and there was a light breeze. And suddenly at the very moment when, so far, I mourned H. least, I remembered her best. Indeed it was something (almost) better than memory; an instantaneous, unanswerable impression. To say it was like a meeting would be going too far. Yet there was that in it which tempts one to use those words. It was as if the lifting of the sorrow removed a barrier.[6]

But There are Relapses!

Lest we conclude from this that Lewis had finally "gotten over" his sorrow, he is quick to remind us that recovery is a process of moving through phases that recur. One never takes steps that leave behind what once was essential to the self and now has been lost. "Tonight all the hells of young grief have opened again; the mad words, the bitter resentment, the fluttering in the stomach, the nightmare unreality, the wallowed-in tears, for in grief nothing 'stays put.' One keeps on emerging from a phase, but it always recurs. . . . They say 'The coward dies many times'; so does the beloved. Didn't the eagle find a fresh liver to tear in Prometheus every time it dined?"[7]

This reminds us that recovery from grief moves through

phases. The recovery of faith is also part of experiencing both the grace of healing and the relapse into grief.

Recovery from grief is more like a spiral with expanding dimensions of healing and hope than a threshold we cross once and for all. We should not think that we have fallen back into hopeless grief when the pangs of a loss or fear of our own death suddenly come upon us after a period of relative peace and well-being. Grieving through to faith is a process by which faith expands through the experience of such pain and fear. To have faith is to be in recovery, even from attacks upon our faith!

Recover Faith in the Face of Suffering

When a person who trusts in God suffers, and is shocked and grieved over the tragedy and pain of others, the recovery of faith is essential to self-recovery. Self-recovery touches the depth of our despair in order to reach the height of our happiness. The self in recovery stretches the boundaries of faith to embrace pain and loss, and strengthens the heart to believe in the meaning and purpose of life.

The young woman dying of cancer discovered that her earlier concepts of God were inadequate to provide her with a foundation of faith and trust in the context of her pain and agony. Her only point of contact with God was her anger and accusation against him. Yet, out of this existential crisis of faith emerged the profile of a suffering God with whom she could identify in her own anguish.

In Christopher Fry's play, *The Boy With a Cart*, Cuthman has been sent by his father out to guard the sheep while they graze. In his simple faith, he talks with God and even has God assist him in guarding the sheep, by drawing a circle around them with his crook. "It is so! Not today only, but other days God took the crook and watched

them in the wind." Informed by a neighbor that his father
has suddenly died, Cuthman is at first disbelieving, and
then defiant. "Let me alone. No; if I come you'll take me
to a place where truth will laugh and scatter like a magpie.
Up here, my father waits for me at home and God sits with
the sheep." After the neighbor leaves, Cuthman expresses
his grief:

> What have I done? Did I steal God away
> From my father to guard my sheep? How can I keep
> Pace with a pain that comes in my head so fast?
> How did I make the day brittle to break?
> What sin brought in the strain, the ominous knock,
> The gaping seam? What have I done to him?
> Father, if you are standing by to help me—
> Help me to cry.

The People of South England, a voice chorus in the play,
chant in unison to Cuthman.

> How is your faith now, Cuthman?
> Your faith that the warm world hatched,
> That spread its unaccustomed colour
> Up on the rock, game and detached?
> You see how sorrow rises, Cuthman,
> How sorrow rises like the heat
> Even up to the plumed hills
> And the quickest feet.
> Pain is low against the ground
> And grows like a weed.
> Is God still in the air
> And in the seed?
> Is God still in the air
> Now that the sun is down?
> They are afraid in the city,

Sleepless in the town,
Cold on the roads,
Desperate by the river.
Can faith for long elude
Prevailing fever?[8]

One role of God in the face of the uncertainty and unpredictability of life is that of assuring that there is some ultimate order and meaning to life. The self cannot really cope with the feeling that life is subject to sheer randomness of disease, destruction and death. If God is no longer in control, then some evil power must lie behind such brutality and horror. If the Devil did not exist, he would have to be invented, in order to provide some explanation for the evil which strikes at the good with such deadly aim. But if we use the Devil to account for evil, what will account for the freedom of this evil one to run rampant over God's good earth and wreak havoc amidst God's children?

In Fry's play, Cuthman returns home, builds a cart, places his mother in a cart pulled by two oxen, and sets off on a pilgrimage of faith to build a church in the place where the "withies" (ropes) which pull the cart break; there he will build the church and work out his grief in thanks to God. He finds compensation and equilibrium in the midst of his carefully constructed world which is crashing down. His story is the crisis of faith and its recovery in the finding of a task which pulls him forward into life.

The human self has within it a capacity for loss and the pain of grief, and also for recovery, for it is endowed with the image of God. The journey of self-recovery is a journey from faith *to* faith.

But how do we begin the journey toward faith? The shocking intrusion of an unexpected and catastrophic loss can appear so irrational and evil that the self's connection with God is broken off at the core. Strange as it may seem, if we hold God ultimately responsible, we may have to begin with forgiving God for what we think He has allowed to happen to us.

Forgive God and Find Faith

Do you remember Susie, my former student and friend? I told her story in Chapter Six. Afflicted with cerebral palsy since birth, she cannot dress or feed herself. She talks with difficulty and in words which emerge as twisted and tortured as the spastic motions required to force them out.

When she received her degree, I had asked her what she intended to do, perceiving her within the boundaries which I had set for her. "Perhaps you will have a significant ministry to others who suffer handicaps in life," I suggested. "No," she said, "most of them haven't forgiven God for who they are, and I have."

The language Susie chose to express her own freedom from blaming God was shocking, but fully in accord with the intimacy with which she talked with God. Instead of nursing inward feelings of self-pity for being a victim of a birth condition, she turned outward toward God as the one who was ultimately responsible for her life. The journey toward faith begins as movement toward God. In Susie's case, instead of blaming God and projecting upon Him feelings of anger and resentment, she sensed that God was grieved with her suffering, even more than was she!

Releasing God from responsibility was her way of receiving God's grace through God's grief. Grace that has not been touched with grief can be meant as kindness but experienced as cruelty.

Susie is one of the most empowered and empowering

persons I know. Just the other day, I encountered her at a conference on shame and grace. "I am engaged," she cried out, thrusting her twisted hand with a ring on it in my direction! As I embraced her and offered my congratulations, she looked at me with a glint in her eye and said, "He thinks I am incredible!" I took it to mean her boyfriend. She might well have meant God!

The Outward Journey toward Inner Healing

In certain instances, Jesus empowered persons through a kind of "transfer of spiritual power." The transfer of spiritual power is not a literal movement of power from one person to another; rather, it is a process of empowerment which results in moral and spiritual health.

When a woman who had suffered years of physical affliction touched the hem of His garment, she was healed instantly. Jesus "felt power go forth from him," and sought her out. When she acknowledged that she had indeed touched Him, despite the "uncleanness" of her medical condition according to the law of Moses, He said, "Daughter, your faith has made you well; go in peace, and be healed of your disease" (Mark 5:34).

Jesus could have said: "See, I do have power to heal, and you were right in touching me." Instead, he attributed her healing to her own faith! He thus empowered her to live out of the wholeness of her own self and to live out of the peace that she was indeed a "daughter" of God.

Self-recovery is not an inward journey, but an outward journey toward inner healing. The journey begins when we discover the growing edge amidst the grieving process.

"You have kept count of my tossings; put my tears in your bottle. Are they not in your record?" (Psalm 56:8)

Who would think of saving tears! They are such unlovely mementos of moments we hasten to forget. Ah, but the value of tears is not to the one who weeps, but to the one who cares.

What would be only a vial of self-pity if kept on the shelf with our other secret treasures, becomes a precious token of shared loneliness—a pledge that the weeping was not desolate nor the pain a barren thorn.

It is not pain that we fear—but barrenness.

The life of the spirit pours out of the open wound that is our heart. The uncontrollable expression of love too long measured out carefully—according to necessity— is a sighing of the body, a spending to be spent.

The pain of this extravagance is not the giving but the undesignated gift. Who is able to receive such an offering?

What green thing grew these tears?[9]

CHAPTER FOURTEEN

Restoration: Living on the Growing Edge

I keep the Lord always before me; because he is at my right hand, I shall not be moved. Therefore my heart is glad, and my soul rejoices; my body also rests secure. . . . You show me the path of life. In your presence there is fullness of joy; in your right hand are pleasures forevermore. (Psalm 16:8-9; 11)

"Wait a minute, I'm not finished yet," was the impatient response from my five-year-old daughter when I once tried to get her to leave her coloring book and come to dinner.

The struggle for recovery is not to overcome the hindrances and problems that beset us *yesterday* and *today,* but to become the person that we will be *tomorrow.* "Wait a minute, I'm not finished yet!"

The goal of recovery is not to emerge from an abusive relationship or traumatic experience as a battle-scarred survivor but as a passionate lover of life. "Wait a minute, I'm not finished yet!"

Recovery is not to be cast as a survivor upon some

deserted beach with the hope that the small island of safety will provide all that is necessary to be self-sufficient. Rather, the gift of recovery is to have the sails repaired, the rudder restored, and one's hand on the tiller with a spanking breeze and a spacious horizon. "Wait a minute, I'm not finished yet!"

From Brokenness to Wholeness

We are fast becoming a society where brokenness can be seen at every hand. Politicians break their promises (Read my lips!), public servants break their trust. Broken marriages, broken families, broken homes, broken lives provide rhetorical thunder for the preachers of traditional values. To rail against brokenness is to rouse the faithful to moral indignation and to make failure into moral tragedy. To be a broken person amidst the scarcity of wholeness is to be told: "Yes, you are finished, whether you know it or not!"

The metaphor of brokenness carries a variety of meanings. Those who suffer through abuse, failed marriages, chemical dependency, moral failure, or excessive grief, are assumed by many to be "broken pieces" floating around the "mainland" of a functionally stable community. Or, to change the metaphor to that of an ocean liner, broken people are like those who fall overboard and are either left to drown or pulled back on ship as a survivor. Even though they have been "recovered," they bear the stigma of being unstable and can never be fully trusted again.

We often refer to people who have gone through a crisis as "broken people." From the outside, it appears that a divorce leaves one a broken person, or that one becomes "broken down" with grief.

Marilyn was a staff member in a Christian organization with an effective ministry of leadership and service. When her marriage failed and a divorce appeared to be imminent, the chief administrator of the organization told her: "You will have to leave because we already have too many broken people around here." Leave she finally did, hurting as much from this rejection as from the failed marriage. As it turned out, the deeper brokenness became the experience of God's power in weakness, His presence for renewal and growth.

Today Marilyn is living on the "growing edge" of life. Meanwhile, the institution which thought that it could not tolerate broken people remains dysfunctional and self-defensive! Its will to survive remains intact, its method is to push broken people overboard if they will not jump.

Those who work in the recovery movement know that growth toward wholeness cannot begin until self-deception and self-justification are broken and the self experiences a vulnerability that creates an opening through which real contact with others can occur. The most difficult movement for the self to make in the recovery process is to experience a real breakdown in the defenses which enabled one to survive as a victim.

Survival is a powerful instinct of self, but it can often hinder growth. The breaking of the self's survival skills in the face of pervasive abuse and punishing loss is a broken edge which is most painful of all. This is the kind of a broken edge, however, where the spirit of renewal and recovery leads to growth.

When recovery produces a creative and growing edge to life, then we know that restoration is occurring.

From Recovery to Restoration

Look with me at David the King. Caught in a moment of sensual vulnerability and royal prerogative, he seduced Bathsheba, the wife of one of his army officers. Her subsequent pregnancy caused him to panic and arrange the murder of her husband as though he were a battle casualty. He thus concealed the incident, took the woman as his wife, and the child was born (2 Samuel 11).

Directed by the Lord, Nathan the Prophet confronted David with the terrible thing that he had done. "I have sinned against the Lord," replied David, when the full extent of his sin and the consequences became clear to him. Nathan reassured him that he would not die, even though the dreadful consequence of the death of the child would ensue (2 Samuel 12).

So much for the incident itself. If there had been no description of the process by which David recovered from this terrible failure, we would read the story as yet another lesson to be learned; when you sin against God you have to suffer the consequences.

"Yes, you are forgiven, David, but for all practical purposes, you are finished."

When I look into the eyes of those who have experienced the shame of being caught in a moral failure I do not often see hope. Even where forgiveness has been offered, restoration of hope does not always result. Forgiveness which does not lead to hope and the recovery of the joy of life is not good enough. The human spirit seeks the recovery of hope even though one is offered formal forgiveness. How can we find restoration and hope when we are flawed beings?

James Leehan suggests that the recognition and articulation of imperfection in one's life can lead to hope rather than despair.

> In a special way, survivors are people of hope.... Hope is the virtue of those who see the imperfection of the present, who recognize the fear, insecurities, and inequalities that exist, and who work for a new order of

things. This recognition of imperfection and its articulation are critical aspects of hope, . . . [1]

The Old Testament theologian, Walter Brueggemann reminds us that " . . . hope emerges among those who publicly articulate and process their grief over their suffering."[2]

This is exactly what David did. In his Psalms David makes public his confession and expresses his confidence in restoration. "While I kept silence," David writes, "my body wasted away through my groaning all day long. . . . Then I acknowledged my sin to you, and I did not hide my iniquity: I said, 'I will confess my transgressions to the Lord,' and you forgave the guilt of my sin" (Psalm 32:3, 5).

In another Psalm, David again acknowledges his sin but goes on to say: "Create in me a clean heart, O God, and put a new and right spirit within me. . . . Restore to me the joy of your salvation, and sustain in me a willing spirit. . . . O Lord, open my lips, and my mouth will declare your praise. For you have no delight in sacrifice. . . . The sacrifice acceptable to God is a broken spirit; a broken and contrite heart, O God, you will not despise" (Psalm 51: 10, 12, 15-17).

"Wait a minute," says David, "I'm not finished yet!"

He discovered the growing edge at the broken edge. David's spirit was not renewed until his self-deception was shattered and he was confronted by the painful reality that his life was exposed before God, even if he thought that it was concealed from others. The painful edge of his brokenness became the creative and growing edge of his renewal and restoration.

With his confession David also prays for restoration. "Restore to me the joy of your salvation," is his prayer. There is no power in the emotional life alone to utter such a prayer and to reach for such a goal. This is the power of the spiritual life of the self under the prompting and empowering of the Spirit of God. Abraham Heschel has reminded us, "In emotion, we are conscious of its being our emotion; in the state of being filled with spirit, we are conscious of joining, sharing or receiving 'spirit from above'.... Passion is a movement; spirit is a goal."[3]

Restoration is a fruit of the Spirit experienced as a creation of new life out of the ruins of the old. Openness to the Spirit of God is often created through the brokenness of our carefully ordered world. We cannot begin to live on the growing edge until we experience spiritual healing for the broken edge.

Restoration for the Innocent Victim

David is an example of a person who found restoration and renewal through his moral and spiritual failure. But what of those who suffer through no fault of their own? What if there is no sin to confess and yet one experiences abuse, tragic loss, and painful suffering?

We have such a person in the case of the prophet Jeremiah. He is assumed by many scholars to be the author of the Old Testament book aptly titled Lamentations. Viewing the fallen city of Jerusalem after the people have been taken into exile, like Jesus centuries later (Luke 19:41), Jeremiah begins his lament by saying:

> How lonely sits the city that once was full of people! How like a widow she has become, she that was great among the nations! She that was a princess among the provinces has become a vassal. She weeps bitterly in the night, with tears on her cheeks; among all her lovers she has no one to comfort her; all her friends have dealt treacherously with her, they have become her enemies. (Lam. 1:1-2)

As he continues his lament over the destruction of Jerusalem, Jeremiah becomes more personal and complains bitterly to the Lord of his own situation.

> I am one who has seen affliction under the rod of God's wrath; he has driven and brought me into darkness without any light; against me alone he turns his hand, again and again, all day long.
>
> He has made my flesh and my skin waste away, and broken my bones; he has besieged and enveloped me with bitterness and tribulation; he has made me sit in darkness like the dead of long ago.
>
> He has walled me about so that I cannot escape; he has put heavy chains on me; though I call and cry for help, he shuts out my prayer; he has blocked my ways with hewn stones, he has made my paths crooked (Lam. 3:1-9).

More than a few suffering souls have found the lament of Jeremiah to ring true to their own experience, though most do not attribute their pain so directly to God in such eloquent fashion. Like Job of old, Jeremiah knows where to lodge his complaint and whom to blame for his condition. But then, as suddenly as it began, it comes to an end.

> The thought of my affliction and my homelessness is
>   wormwood and gall!
> My soul continually thinks of it
>   and is bowed down within me.
> But this I call to mind, and therefore I have hope:
>
> The steadfast love of the Lord never ceases,
>   his mercies never come to an end;
> They are new every morning;
>   great is your faithfulness.
> "The Lord is my portion," says my soul,
>   "therefore I will hope in him."   (Lam. 3:19-24)

Many Christians cheerfully sing the hymn, "Great is Thy Faithfulness," without realizing the anguish which brought forth such assurance. This could be the searching sweep of the Spirit reaching deep through layers of emotion to touch the brokenhearted. How much we need to connect with the source of this affirmation of trust and confidence in God!

In a way that is very similar to that of King David, the process of recovery and restoration for Jeremiah begins with a confession of pain, an address to God (prayer), followed by the gift of a new spirit and restored hope in God. Like David, this process is part of a communal experience and expression, with an utterance that breaks out of the private world of the self into shared life with others.

Restoration for the Broken In Spirit

The circumstances which cause one to suffer pain and distress of soul may be quite different. For some it comes as a result of their own actions, for others as a victim of abuse or the blind and senseless ravages of natural life. In a very remarkable way, however, the process of recovery and restoration is quite similar. We can become broken in spirit through the abuse of others just as surely as through our own failure and foolishness.

But herein lies a profound truth.

The brokenness of the human spirit is a deeper and more creative edge than guilt and remorse for sin. A sense of guilt is not creative and produces no positive motivation toward spiritual wholeness. We tend to forget that the cross of Christ only has significance as a place where sin is judged for those who have experienced the power of resurrection and the gift of the Spirit of God. It is true, consciousness of sin can lead to brokenness of spirit and thus to healing and wholeness.

But so does the brokenness of spirit resulting from abuse, pain, and suffering! Those of us who are victims of the abuse of others also need healing for our bruised hearts and redemption of our broken spirit. The suffering of Christ avails for us too as it does for all who are innocent victims of life's injustice and cruelty.

There is no need to make people whose spirit is broken feel condemned as a condition for receiving grace. In fact, this may well bruise the broken spirit and turn what could be a hopeful spiritual experience of recovery of the joy of salvation into a hopeless inward spiral of self-condemnation.

"The Lord is near to the broken hearted," wrote David, "and saves the crushed in Spirit" (Psalm 34:18). God's touch is firm, but light. His Spirit is powerful but not violent. "A bruised reed he will not break, and a dimly burning wick he will not quench" (Isaiah 42:3).

The spiritual goal for the broken spirit is renewal and restoration through the power of God. This is the gift of God which comes freely to those who receive the Spirit. "For all who are led by the Spirit of God are children of God.... When we cry 'Abba! Father!' it is that very Spirit bearing witness with our spirit that we are children of God, ..." (Rom. 8:14-16).

In the parable of the Prodigal Son, the son was not broken in spirit by the desperate conditions in the far country, where he was reduced to living with the swine. He returned home with a confession upon his lips but with no joy in his heart. He thought that his life as a son was finished for good, and he was prepared to live in his father's house as a servant. Instead, the father rushed out and kissed him, and proclaimed, "This son of mine was dead and is alive again; he was lost and is found!" (Luke 15:24)

The broken edge was not due to the son's failure to achieve what he set out to do, but to the damaged relationship which only the father could restore. The human spirit is nurtured by relationships not by rules. When we break the rules we suffer the consequences. When we experience a broken relationships we suffer a broken edge of the spirit.

The broken edge of the relationship with the father became a creative opportunity for the son to become what he had not yet achieved—a life of sonship with an openness to the future. It was there, at the broken edge that the growing edge of recovery and restoration began. Restoration is the recovery of the spiritual power of our lives to become the person that God intended.

From Overcoming to Becoming

"Spirituality for survivors is a topic that needs much work in the future," writes James Leehan. "Survivors do not need an emphasis on evil and sin; they have gotten more than enough of that. As victims they were constantly told how wicked and bad they were, and as survivors they are struggling to overcome that image."[4]

The effect of suffering, pain, and experience of loss upon the self is a narrowing one. Anxiety causes the self to tighten up. The flow of blood is restricted. Muscular movements become stiff and constricted. The self retreats into isolation and sets up defenses against the intrusion of further pain. The Latin word for anxiety is *angustia*, a word which means narrowness. The first step toward recovery is to overcome the effects of this constriction of the self and to emerge into the larger space of self-expression and relation with others.[5]

The deep feelings experienced during intense pain and

suffering may actually be a narrowing of the flow of emotions by the denial of the full range of feelings which contribute to the health and creative life of the self.

Growth toward full restoration of creative life builds on the overcoming of the constricting force of anxiety produced by suffering and pain. Overcoming is like crawling out of a raging river gorge which threatens to carry us downstream to our destruction. Having escaped the force of the stream that seeks to pull us under, we have become a survivor.

Overcoming in order to be a survivor, however, is not enough. To think of oneself as a survivor may empower the self emotionally and lead to recovery, but it fails to satisfy the deeper yearnings and possibility of the self. Survivors may have conquered an addiction, learned to let go of a tragic loss, escaped from dysfunctional relationships, and be healed of traumatic abuse, but this is still not enough.

Beyond overcoming is becoming. More than emotional repair is needed. We have not fully recovered until the abundant spiritual life of fellowship with God and relation with others is restored. Restoration is the fullness of God creating anew a spiritual dimension.

Perhaps we have never experienced this fullness. Or, we have only experienced the longing for it. Each of us has the God-given capacity for becoming what we were created to be. Even our unfulfilled longing is a witness to this capacity. Restoration begins with opening up this capacity and then moving us toward fulfillment. This is the experience of God's gracious Spirit working with our spirit.

It is the spiritual core of the self which gives direction to the emotions and expands the creative capacity of the self. When the irrepressible spirit of creativity, imagination, and vision is unleashed within us, we move away from the security of a fixed center toward the growing edge. It is our spiritual life of faith, hope and love that enables the self to transcend its narrowness, to move beyond its own history, and create its own story.

It is the spirit in us that cries out, "Wait a minute, I'm not finished yet!"

Living on the Growing Edge

The spiritual dimension in recovery begins where the broken edge becomes the growing edge. All brokenness brings emotional pain for which there is no rational relief. The healing of emotional pain is the spiritual work of the self. Growth does not come through emotional change alone, but through the life of the spirit. It is the spirit which expands the self and directs the self toward growth. The feelings of the self are the core of subjectivity and individuality. The spirit of the self constitutes the openness of the self to the spirit of others and, essentially and ultimately to the Spirit of God.

The self *overcomes* obstacles and hindrances through the power of will driven by sufficient emotional resources. But the self *becomes* through spirit, and expands in growth as recovery toward the reality that faith and hope envision.

Growth is Openness to Change

A healthy self is one that is in balance and capable of growth. A growing self is dynamic and flexible, able to absorb shock, to make adjustments under stress, and to shift the self's center of gravity in order to maintain balance. Traumatic shock and grievous loss can produce emotional rigidity—the self's desperate attempt to maintain balance and control under trauma and stress.

When the self is fearful it takes a negative direction, pulling back from shock and refusing to deal with the change which comes about through unexpected events and sudden losses. The self attempts to restore its familiar sense of order by locating a known center that is secure and safe. This coping mechanism of withdrawal is sometimes the only defense left to a person in an abusive relationship. When the abuse is inevitable, but unpredictable, the self creates an inner refuge from the violence, much as a person living amidst urban terrorism places iron bars on the windows and cowers inside.

We often think of emotional trauma and pain as a state of disorder in the self. Actually, emotional pain and a dysfunctional relationship constitute the most stable of all systems, and the least susceptible to change. To introduce change into a rigid emotional structure of the self only stiffens the resistance.

Persons who experience the devastating loss of a marriage or the death of a loved one often find it difficult to deal with the shock of losing something which had become so much a part of self-identity. Like an earthquake fault that splits one's house in two, a sudden and traumatic loss is a seismic shudder which can cause the self to retreat from the fault line of pain in order to stop the tremors.

This attempt at recovery retreats from the broken edge in search of a space which is under control and not subject to change. The paradox is that change is a break in the established pattern and produces momentary disequilibrium in the rigid structure of the self. Before change and growth can occur, the structure of the self must shift from a rigid to a dynamic and flexible state. This requires a strongly supportive environment so that sufficient balance and stability is provided for the self while experiencing the stress and "shifting of the ground" under one's feet.

Openness to the spirit of others and to supportive relationships is crucial to a process of growth and change.
Self-recovery means the recovery of the self in relationships, sustained by a spiritual openness to love, faith and
hope. This is the recovery of the original form of the self
as created in the image and likeness of God.

Openness to change is a characteristic of the self which
is on the growing edge of life. When brokenness occurs, as
it does to all of us, it presents a crisis to the self. Healthy
recovery goes through the shock and trauma of pain and
loss, but discovers the resources to adjust to the shock and
adapt to the change. This is the spiritual aspect of self-
recovery, for the self experiences a revitalization of spirit
which produces the gift of faith and hope. The reach of the
human spirit to the Spirit of God underlies the self's capacity for faith, hope, and ultimately trust and acceptance.

The Apostle Paul had a remarkable openness to change,
and therefore to growth, in his life, primarily due to the fact
that he experienced a shattering loss of all that he had
attempted to build up as a self-righteous member of the
religious sect of the Pharisees. Through his encounter with
the resurrected Jesus Christ on the road to Damascus (Acts
9), Paul received the gift of a new spirit of faith and life.
While others of his contemporaries found it difficult to let
go of the rituals and rules by which they had formerly
lived, Paul, led by the Spirit of Christ, lived on the growing
edge.

Years later, when he experienced a physical illness,
which he called a "thorn in the flesh," he sought healing
and relief through prayer. After appealing to the Lord
three times, he received his answer, "My grace is sufficient
for you, for power is made perfect in weakness" (2 Cor.
12:8-9).

The growing edge of life is where openness to change

becomes a form of spiritual empowerment. In Christ, Paul reminds us, "everything has become new!" though not everything is possible (2 Cor. 5:17).

I think that there is a special gift of the Spirit where life becomes broken. The power made manifest in weakness is the filling of the self with the Spirit of God. When our feelings are numb to that possibility, and our emotions rage against the Spirit, we can dare to say, "Wait a minute, I'm not finished yet!"

Growth is an Interchange of Life in Community

The growth of the self is not an individual process. We are each created as unique persons. We come to experience and discover this uniqueness in relation to others. Even as an infant experiences selfhood and self-identity through encounters with others, the growth of the self continues throughout life via social interchange.

With brokenness there is bleeding. Every hurt and each loss is a hemorrhage through which the self bleeds its pain. Left to ourselves, we attempt to staunch the flow as best we can. After a time, the wound seems to be healed, and the pain subsides. Then suddenly, like an aftershock of an earthquake long forgotten, a tremor arises within us and the hurt spills over again, an embarrassment to us and a discomfort for others.

Healed over pain is like a hidden land mine, one misstep and it blows up right in your face. We should never walk alone in the pathway of recovery. We need companions who have walked that way before and who are safe escorts.

Here we discover the double bind in moving from recovery toward restoration. Without the supportive and affirming experience of others we walk alone like lonely survivors in a crowd. At the same time, it is often through those whom we have trusted and those to whom we have looked for support that we have received injury and abuse.

Life in relation to others is no protection against abuse, pain and tragic loss. In fact, shared promises and commitments raises the stakes of our losses and griefs.

There is something in us that wants to avoid this by withholding commitment and reserving our independence. But solitariness (not solitude!) is a form of abuse for the human spirit. And walking alone provides no certainty of never falling.

"Two are better than one," wrote the ancient Preacher, "because they have a good reward for their toil. For if they fall, one will lift up the other; but woe to one who is alone and falls and does not have another to help" (Eccl. 4:9-10).

There are people who have walked the road to recovery and who have been restored. These are the ones who can serve as escorts for our own journey.

When we experience brokenness within a community of support and care, there is an interchange, a transfusion, so that what life flows out of us flows back into us, filtered through the fabric of intentional care. Within the life of the self in relation to others, there flows the pain of others as well as the joy of others.

The apostle Paul was fond of the metaphor of the human body to express the relationships which Christians have bound together in Christ. "For just as the body is one and has many members, and all the members of the body, though many, are one body, so it is with Christ" (1 Cor. 12:12). As each part of the body has its life through the interconnection and interchange with the other parts, so it is with the individual as a member of the community of Christ.

In his letter to the Ephesian church, Paul is even more

graphic in using this metaphor to explain the interchange of life necessary to healthy growth and life. "But speaking the truth in love, we must grow up in every way into him who is the head, into Christ, from whom the whole body, joined and knit together by every ligament with which it is equipped, as each part is working properly, promotes the body's growth in building itself up in love" (Eph. 4:15-16).

The experience of brokenness and the creative power of spirit takes place within the life of the body and the care which members have for one another. "If one member suffers, all suffer with it; if one member is honored, all rejoice together with it" (1 Cor. 12:26).

"Wait a minute," my daughter said, "I'm not finished yet." We did wait. And what do we have to show for it? Not a finished page in a coloring book—that was long discarded! We have a family, where no one is quite finished but where everyone is looking forward to completeness. I believe that's called recovery.

Notes

Introduction

[1]*A Sleep of Prisoners* (London: Oxford University Press, 1951), p. 49.

Chapter One

[1]Archibald Hart, *Unlocking the Mystery of Your Emotions* (Dallas: Word Publishing, 1989).

[2]Opal Whiteley, *Opal—The Journal of an Understanding Heart.* Adapted by Jane Boulton (Palo Alto: Tiogo Publishing Company, 1984), pp. 45-46.

[3]Annie Dillard, *An American Childhood* (Harper and Row, 1987), p. 11.

Chapter Two

[1]"The emotional life is not simply a part or an aspect of life. It is not, as we so often think, subordinate, or subsidiary to the mind. It is the core and essence of human life. The intellect arises out of it, is rooted in it, draws its nourishment and sustenance from it, and is the subordinate partner in the human economy. This is because the intellect is essentially instrumental. Thinking is not living. At its worst it is a substitute for living; at its best a means of living better. As we have seen, the emotional life is our life, both as awareness of the world and as action in the world, so far as it is lived for its own

sake. Its value lies in itself, not in anything beyond it which it is a means of achieving." John Macmurray, *Reason and Emotion* (London: Faber and Faber, 1935), p. 75.

[2]John Macmurray, *Reason and Emotion*, pp. 49-50.

[3]"Genuine feeling, as for instance sorrow or joy, is not possible without spirit. For such feelings arise only out of or in spiritual connections. A good meal does not arouse joy; it merely gives pleasure; if I eat with joy it is because my spirit is turned in a certain direction, to that which is true, or good, or beautiful, which is connected with the act of eating, as indeed the Apostle is able to say: 'whether ye eat or drink, do all to the glory of God.' Through joy pleasure is lifted to a higher plane since its subject is understood in a larger context." E. Brunner, *Man in Revolt* (Philadelphia: Westminster Press, 1979, reprint [London: Lutterworth Press, 1939]), p. 251.

[4]A. Heschel, *The Prophets*, Vol. II (New York: Harper and Row, 1962), pp. 96-97.

[5]Mary Vander Goot, *Healthy Emotions: Helping Children Grow* (Grand Rapids: Baker Book House, 1987), p. 43.

[6]Wolfhart Pannenberg, *Anthropology in Theological Perspective* (Philadelphia: Westminster Press, 1985), p. 259.

Chapter Three

[1]Vander Goot, *Healthy Emotions: Helping Children Grow*), p. 23.

[2]"The view that emotions cannot be changed, or can be changed only slightly, is false. It is now known that emotions, to a large extent, involve thought. Therefore, we can change our emotions by changing our thought. We can even learn how to change from being an angry person to hardly ever being angry. We can change our entire personalities in this way. We can eliminate negative emotions (jealousy, anger, envy, etc.) and develop positive emotions such as warmth, love, being happy, enjoying humor, etc." Warren Shibles, *Emotion: The Method of Philosophical Therapy* (Whitewater, Wisconsin: The Language Press, 1974), pp. 17-19.

[3]Prior to much of the left/right brain research, William James suggested forms of consciousness which lie outside of the normal thought process. "Our normal waking consciousness, rational consciousness, as we call it, is but one special type of consciousness, whilst all about it, parted from it by the filmiest [sic] of screens, there

lie potential forms of consciousness entirely different. We may go through life without suspecting their existence; but apply the requisite stimulus, and at a touch they are there in all their completeness, definite types of mentality which probably somewhere have their field of application and adaptation." Betty Edwards, *The Varieties of Religious Experience*. Cited in *Drawing on the Right Side of the Brain* (Los Angeles: J. P. Tarcher, Inc., 1979), p. 46.

[4]John Pedersen, *Israel: Its Life and Culture,* Vol. 1. (London: Oxford University Press, 1973), p. 107.

[5]"We are told we must release our emotions or tell what we really feel inside us. The picture of 'release' and of emotions as things 'inside us,' is damaging and unhelpful. It creates the view that we are irrational and that there are evil forces within us at work which we can do little about except to let these 'forces' be released now and again as water is released from a dam....To 'release' emotions is not to effect a cure, but in fact is to create a harmful pattern of behavior." Warren Shibles, *Emotion: The Method of Philosophical Therapy*, pp. 217, 218.

Chapter Four

[1]The Christian psychologist, Craig Ellison, offers a definition that includes the elements of self concept and implies positive self-worth by suggesting that self-esteem results from a comparison between the perceived self and the ideal self. "The most commonly accepted analysis of self-esteem sees it as the result of comparisons between one's perceived self, which combines both the assessments of others and one's private perceptions, and the ideal self, which is both how one feels one would like to be and how one feels one ought to be." Craig Ellison, *Your Better Self: Christianity, Psychology, and Self-Esteem* (New York: Harper and Row, 1983), p. 3.

[2]Archibald Hart, *Unlocking the Mystery of Your Emotions* (Dallas: Word Publishing, 1989), p. 94 .

[3]Arthur Miller, "Death of a Salesman" in *Arthur Miller's Collected Plays*, Volume I (New York: The Viking Press, 1957, 1987), pp. 221-222.

[4]*Toward a State of Self-Esteem*. The Final Report of the California Task Force to Promote Self-Esteem and Personal and Social Responsibility, January, 1990.

[5]"The sense of loss and diminished self-esteem attack the fundamental narcissism at the root of our emotional lives. This narcissism is essential to our psychological well-being and any threat to it must be resisted. And so loss sets in motion restorative efforts by which the ego strives to recover the loss and reconstitute the sense of self-esteem. Self-esteem is a fragile but indispensable vessel, whose preservation requires care and constant effort in the fact of the onslaughts of deprivation and loss." W. W. Meissner, *Life and Faith* (Washington, D.C.: University of Georgetown Press, 1987), p. 140.

[6]"Embracing a positive image of self will not, in the long run, make any difference, because I am still wrapped up in myself. Even if I feel bad about myself and do not like myself, I am still focusing upon myself and 'myself' is the problem. The corrupted condition of my human 'self' is not a mere figment of imagination which can be adjusted by thinking differently....The call of the Gospel is away from self and unto Jesus, because *self is the problem and Jesus is the solution.*" Don Matzat, *Christ Esteem—Where the Search for Self-Esteem Ends* (Eugene, OR: Harvest House Publishers, 1990), pp. 71-72.

[7]*I and Thou*, tr. by Walter Kaufman (Edinburgh: T. & T. Clark, 1979), p. 62.

[8]*Persons in Relation* (London: Faber and Faber, 1961), p. 150.

[9]"God, who inclined toward his new-born creature with infinite personal love, in order to inspire him with it and to awaken the response to it in him, does in the divine supernatural order something similar to a mother. Out of the strength of her own heart she awakens love in her child in true creative activity.... The essential thing is that the child, awakened thus to love, and already endowed by another's power of love, awakens also to himself and to his true freedom, which is in fact the freedom of loving transcendence of his narrow individuality. No man reaches the core and ground of his own being, becoming free to himself and to all beings, unless love shines on him." Hans Urs von Balthasar, *A Theological Anthropology* (New York: Sheed and Ward, 1967), p. 87.

Chapter Five

[1]"If survivors of abuse seek pastoral counseling and again are told not be angry, they are being told that they are not worth caring

about.... We must accept and even encourage their anger as an appropriate response to the injustice that has been done to them. We must support their feelings and share our own anger about the way they have been mistreated." James Leehan, *Pastoral Care for Survivors of Family Abuse* (Louisville: Westminster Press, 1989), pp. 97-98.

[2]"Moral rules are based on a primitive level of development. They are derived from fear, a response to threats of abandonment, punishment, exposure, or the inner threat of guilt, shame, or isolation. Ethical rules, however, are based on ideals to be striven for.... There is a violence inherent in the moral sense." Meissner, *Life and Faith*, pp. 249; 252.

Chapter Six

[1]James Leehan, *Pastoral Care for Survivors of Family Abuse*, p. 90.

Chapter Seven

[1]Dietrich Bonhoeffer, *Life Together* (London: SCM Press, 1970), pp. 115-116.

[2]*Sand and Foam—A Book of Aphorisms* (New York: Alfred A. Knopf, 1964), p. 24.

Chapter Eight

[1]Ridgely, Torrence, *Miami Poets: Percy MacKaye and Ridgely Torrence*, edited by William Pratt (Oxford, Ohio: Miami University, 1988), p. 64.

Chapter Nine

[1]Theodore Roszak, *Person/Planet* (Garden City, NY: Doubleday, 1979), pp. 139, 142.

[2]Abraham J. Heschel, reminds us that the frequent references to the wrath or anger of God must be understood within the aspect of the pathos of God. "The anger of God must not be treated in isolation, but

as an aspect of the divine pathos, as one of the modes of God's responsiveness to man....For all the terror that the wrath of God may bring upon man, the prophet is not crushed or shaken in his understanding and trust. What is divine is never weird. This is the greatness of the prophet: he is able to convert terror into a song. For when the Lord smites the Egyptians, he is both 'smiting and healing' (Isa. 19:22)....The divine pathos, whether mercy or anger, was never thought of as an impulsive act, arising automatically within the divine Being as the reaction to man's behavior and as something due to peculiarity of temperament or propensity. It is neither irrational nor irresistible. Pathos results from a decision, from an act of will. It comes about in the light of moral judgment rather than in the darkness of passion." *The Prophets*, Volume II (New York: Harper and Row, 1962), pp. 63, 78.

[3]Theodore Roszak, *Person/Planet,* p. 167.

[4]C. S. Lewis "Relapse," from *C. S. Lewis' Poems* (New York: Harcourt, Brace and World, 1964), p. 103.

Chapter Ten

[1]Sociologists Richard Gelles and Murray Straus state it as plainly as can be said: "You are more likely to be physically assaulted, beaten, and killed in your own home at the hands of a loved one than any place else, or by any one else in our society....In our society, a person's earliest experiences with violence comes in the home—spankings and physical punishment from parents. We learn that there is always going to be a certain amount of violence that accompanies intimacy." Richard J. Gelles and Murray A. Straus, *Intimate Violence: The Causes and Consequences of Abuse in the American Family,* (New York: Simon and Schuster, 1988), pp. 18, 20-21.

[2]*Time,* June 29, 1992, p. 57.

[3]Gelles and Straus, *Intimate Violence,* p. 51.

[4]Gelles and Straus, *Intimate Violence,* p. 43. "Initially, the response to family violence was to assume that abusive family members were mentally ill. But over the past two decades the tendency to diagnose the causes of violence as a psychological abnormality or mental illness has declined. We realize now that individual psychiatric care for violent family members is but one limited treatment for the problem. Since the roots of family violence lie in the structure of

the family and society, we know that individual psychiatric treatment can be effective with only a small number of cases of violence and abuse." Ibid., p. 128.

[5]Gelles and Cornell distinguish between normal and abusive violence: "Normal violence is the commonplace pushes, shoves, and spankings that frequently are considered a normal or accepted part of raising children or interacting with a spouse.... The more dangerous acts of violence we shall refer to as 'abusive violence.' These acts are defined as acts that have the high potential for injuring the person being hit." Richard J. Gelles and Claire Pedrick Cornell, *Intimate Violence in Families*—Family Study Series # 2 (Newbury Park, CA: Sage Publications, 1985), pp. 22-3.

However, Gelles and Strauss, in a later book, appear to abandon this distinction: "Our view is that it is impossible to distinguish between force and violence. Rather, all violent acts—from pushing and shoving to shooting and stabbing—properly belong under a single definition of violence.... In reality, true insight into the nature of violence requires us to shed our stereotypes and blinders about routine spankings, normal pushings, and seemingly harmless grabbings, and to see these acts as part of the problem of intimate violence." *Intimate Violence,* 1988, pp. 54-55.

[6]Gelles and Cornell, *Intimate Violence in Families,* p. 76.

[7]One of the most insightful and helpful treatments of recovery from traumatic and abusive experiences can be found in Judith Lewis Herman, M.D., *Trauma and Recovery: The Aftermath of Violence— From Domestic Abuse to Political Terror* (New York: Basic Books, 1992). "Recovery," writes Dr. Herman, "can take place only in the context of relationships; it cannot occur in isolation. In her renewed connections with other people, the survivor re-creates the psychological faculties that were damaged or deformed by the traumatic experience.... Just as these capabilities are originally formed in relationships with other people, they must be reformed in such relationships." p. 133.

[8]A. Heschel, *The Prophets,* Vol. II (New York: Harper and Row, 1962), pp. 96-97.

[9]*Trauma and Recovery: The Aftermath of Violence—From Domestic Abuse to Political Terror,* p. 133.

[10]Ray S. Anderson, *The Gospel According to Judas* (Colorado Springs: Helmers and Howard Publishers, 1991), p. 125.

Chapter Eleven

[1]Lewis B. Smedes, *Shame and Grace—Healing the Shame We Don't Deserve* (San Francisco: Harper/San Francisco, 1993), p. 41.

[2]Robert Karen, "Shame," *The Atlantic Monthly*, Volume 269, No. 2, February 1992, p. 41.

[3]John Bradshaw, *Bradshaw On: Healing the Shame that Binds You* (Deerfield Beach, FL: Health Communications, Inc., 1988), p. vii. "Healthy shame keeps us grounded. It is a yellow light warning us that we are essentially limited. *Healthy shame is the basic metaphysical boundary for human beings*. It is the emotional energy which signals us that we are not God—that we have made and will make mistakes, that we need help," p. 4.

[4]*Shame and Grace—Healing the Shame We Don't Deserve*, p. 31.

[5]Ibid., p. 42.

[6]Ibid., p. 35.

[7]The theologian C. Norman Kraus says, "In no way can shame be expiated through substitutionary compensation or retaliation....Only a forgiveness which covers the past and a genuine restoration of relationship can banish shame. What is needed is a restoration of communication. The rage which isolates and insulates must be overcome. Reconciliation and restoration of mutual intimate relationship through a loving open exchange is the only way to heal resentment and restore lost self-esteem." *Jesus Christ our Lord—Christology From a Disciple's Perspective* (Scottdale, PA: Herald Press, 1987), p. 211.

[8]Robert Karen, "Shame," *The Atlantic Monthly*, p. 47.

[9]*Shame and Grace—Healing the Shame We Don't Deserve*, p. 116.

[10]Robert Karen, "Shame," *The Atlantic Monthly*, pp. 42-43.

[11]Ibid., p. 47.

[12]John Bradshaw. *Bradshaw On: Healing the Shame that Binds You,* p. 10.

[13]Ibid., p. 26.

[14]I have adapted these three concepts from Bradshaw, p. 135, but have added my own commentary.

[15]Insightful use of the Adam and Eve story as a metaphor for shame and recovery can be found in the book by Curtis Levang, *The Adam and Eve Complex—Freedom from the Shame That Can*

Separate You from God, Others, and Yourself (Minneapolis: CompCare Books, 1992).

[16]*Shame and Grace—Healing the Shame We Don't Deserve*, p. 119. "The effect of grace is not to eliminate healthy shame but to eliminate its threat. The threat is the possibility of being rejected. Once grace cancels that possibility, the pain of shame is easier to bear." p. 154.

[17]I have discussed the dynamics of this process of discovery, when transformation actually occurs through the motive power of love and the role of the counselor as mediator in, *Christians Who Counsel—The Vocation of Wholistic Therapy* (Grand Rapids: Zondervan, 1990), pp. 67ff.

[18]As a case study in recovery from shame and self-condemnation, I wrote the book, *The Gospel According to Judas* (Colorado Springs: Helmers and Howard, 1991). For some suggested steps toward recovery, see pp. 151ff.

[19]For practical help in stopping self-shaming habits and deflecting the shaming words and actions of others, I recommend the book by Curtis Levang, *The Adam and Eve Complex—Freedom from the Shame that Can Separate You from God, Others, and Yourself* (Minneapolis: CompCare Books, 1992), especially pp. 79-87.

Chapter Twelve

[1]"Within the Wave," in *The Unicorn* (New York: Pantheon Books, 1956), p. 78.

[2]Richard F. Vieth, *Holy Power, Human Pain* (Bloomington, IN: Meyer-Stone Books, 1988), p. 106.

[3]For further exploration of the dynamics of betrayal see my book, *The Gospel According to Judas*.

[4]A reference to the book by Paul Tillich, *The Courage to Be* (London: Collins, 1962).

[5]Arthur Miller, *After the Fall*, in *Arthur Miller's Collected Plays*, Volume II, p. 190.

[6]Anne Morrow Lindberg, "Second Sowing," in *The Unicorn* (New York: Pantheon Books, 1956), p. 32.

Chapter Thirteen

[1]For an insightful treatment of divine power and human suffering see, Richard F. Vieth, *Holy Power, Human Pain* (Bloomington, IN: Meyer-Stone Books, 1988).

[2]Dietrich Bonhoeffer, *Letters and Papers from Prison*—New Greatly Enlarged Edition (New York: Macmillan, 1971), pp. 360-61.

[3]Harold S. Kushner, *When Bad Things Happen to Good People* (New York: Avon Books, 1981), p. 134.

[4]S. Paul Schilling, *God and Human Anguish* (Nashville: Abingdon, 1977), p. 10.

[5]C. S. Lewis, *A Grief Observed* (London: Faber and Faber, 1961), p. 44.

[6]C. S. Lewis, *A Grief Observed*, p. 57.

[7]Ibid., p. 46.

[8]Christopher Fry, *The Boy With a Cart* (New York: Oxford University Press, 1959), pp. 6, 7.

[9]Ray S. Anderson, *The Love That God Is*, unpublished journal notes, August, 1963.

Chapter Fourteen

[1]James Leehan, *Pastoral Care for Survivors of Family Abuse* (Louisville: Westminster/John Knox Press, 1989), p. 101.

[2]Walter Brueggemann, *Hope Within History* (Atlanta: John Knox Press, 1987), p. 84.

[3]*The Prophets*, Vol. II, p. 97.

[4]James Leehan, *Pastoral Care for Survivors of Family Abuse,* pp. 99, 100.

[5]By overcoming the anxiety (narrowness) imposed upon them, survivors will confront the questions life has presented (an important part of the first movement of the spiritual life), let go of their anger (the forgiveness involved in the second movement), and be freed to receive new life from the God of all life." James Leehan, *Pastoral Care for Survivors of Family Abuse*, p. 114.

About the Author

RAY S. ANDERSON is a master storyteller and widely respected writer in the emerging field of integrative theology and psychology. A popular teacher at Fuller Seminary in Pasadena, CA, Anderson is also pastor of Harbour Fellowship in Huntington Beach, California. Based on vigorous scholarship (Ph.D., New College, Edinburgh), Anderson offers fresh perspectives on the soul's search to put faith and life in balance, to make living on the edge possible and desirable.

Other books by Dr. Anderson include *Self-Care, Everything I Needed to Know I Learned from My Father, The Gospel According to Judas* and *Everything that Makes Me Unhappy I Learned as a Child.*